Memories and Nightmares

My Life In Freedom,
As A Japanese POW,
and
My Free Life Afterward
***THE TRUE STORY OF
JOHN JACOB HUMMEL***

*Compiled and Written by
B.J. Bryan*

Copyrights and Credits:

Title- Memories and Nightmares
Author–B.J. Bryan
Memories and Nightmares Text copyright © 2015
All domestic and international copyrights apply.
All Copyright ©2015

No part of this publication may be reproduced, stored in a retrieval system, transmitted in any form, or by any form, electronic, mechanical, photocopying, recording, or otherwise, without the written permission of the Publisher Beautiful Wrinkles Press.
ISBN(13) 978-069-2736-86-9
ISBN (10) 069-2736867
BISAC: HIS016000 United States /Historiography

Printed in the United States of America

First Edition First Printing 2016

DEDICATION

Dedicated To:
Those Families Who Had POWs Return Home
Who Would Not, Or Could Not Talk.
Perhaps This Will Ease Your Mind Somewhat
When You See What Other POWs Went Through;
And Also Dedicated To The Memory
Of Those POWs
Who Made The Supreme Sacrifice

Table Of Contents

Foreword / I Am The Flag	i
My Life In Freedom	1
Uncle Sam Calls	7
War!	23
Bataan	37
Bataan Death March	55
Corregidor	57
Prisoner Of War	67
Cabanatuan Prison Of War Camp	73
Tanagawa Prison Of War Camp	87
Zentsuji Prison Of War Camp	109
The Year 1944	121
1944 And 1945	145
Roku Roshi Prison Of War Camp	149
Japan Surrenders	155
Freedom At Last	165
Good Old U.S.A.!	169
Japanese Prison Guards	183
Acknowlegements	213
Author Biography	215

Foreword

B.J.'s latest book is a fascinating view of World War II from the men who fought it. It is based on a diary kept by a young First Lieutenant in the Indiana National Guard fresh out of college and commanding a platoon in an Armor Company.

As he is courting his future wife, he is ordered to join his unit with another and report to San Francisco, and duty overseas. His frantic efforts to marry his beloved, drives to California in a car with bad tires in the winter of 1941, and prepares for possible war is something only a love-struck pair could accomplish.

His arrival at Clark Field in the Philippines weeks beforethe attack on Pearl Harbor, gives the reader a close up look at the lack of readiness of the U.S. Army for war. He notes the confusion and lack of preparation by the command structure. At the same time it reveals the military's belief that war with Japan was imminent. Yet exercises and target practice are not mentioned by Lt. Hummel.

Foreward

There is also an interesting mystery raised by the book. Why were Lt. Hummel's tanks first issued ammunition the night before Pearl Harbor and the Philippines were attacked?

Before long Lt. Hummel is huddled in a cave, his tanks destroyed, and with little food on Corregidor. His diary details the hardships that follow the flight of General McArthur and the abandoning of the Philippines and our soldiers … the Bataan Death March, the rigors of Japanese prison camps, and notes the many violations of the Geneva Convention in the camps by the guards.

Most fascinating was the ingenuity and determination of prisoners to survive and support their comrades. It is a fresh look at a terrible war from the point of view of a soldier whose fight was not with guns, but wits and courage but who suffered nonetheless!

Michael Miles
Staff Sergeant
U. S. Army Reserve (Ret.)

I Am The Flag

I am the flag of the United States of America; My name is Old Glory.

I fly atop the worlds tallest buildings. I stand watch in America's Halls of Justice

I fly majestically over institutions of learning. I stand guard with power in the world.

Look up and see me!

I stand for peace, honor, truth, and justice. I stand for freedom.

I am confident. I am arrogant. I am proud. When I am flown with my fellow banners,

My head is a little higher; my colors a little truer.

I bow to no one! I am recognized all over the world.
I am worshipped. I am saluted. I am loved. I am revered.
I am respected and I am feared.

I Am The Flag

I have fought in every battle of every war for more than 200 years.

I was flown at Valley Forge, Gettysburg, Shiloh, and Appomattox.

I was there at San Juan Hill, the trenches of France, in the Argonne Forest,

Anzio, Rome, and the beaches of Normandy, Guam, Okinawa, Korea,

Khe San, Saigon, Vietnam, Iraq, Afghanistan; they all know me.

I was there! Troops, I was dirty, battle-tested, and tired,

But my soldiers cheered me and I was proud.

America has been attacked by cowardly fanatics and many lives have been lost.

But those who would destroy me cannot win for I am the symbol of Freedom.

One nation, Under God, Indivisible, With Liberty, and Justice for all.

I have been burned, torn, and trampled on the streets of my country.

And when it's by those whom I've served in battle, it hurts.

But I shall overcome for I am strong.

I have slipped the bonds of Earth and stood over the uncharted frontiers of space

From my vantage point on the moon.

I have borne silent witness to all of America's finest hours.

But my finest hours are yet to come.

When I am torn into strips and used as bandages for my wounded comrades on the battlefield, when I am flown at half-mast to honor my soldier,
Or when I lie in the trembling arms of a grieving parent at the grave of their
Fallen son or daughter, I am proud.

MY NAME IS OLD GLORY
LONG MAY I WAVE.

Chapter 1
My Life In Freedom

I was born 11 December 1919, in Mayfield, Washington to Jasper Oliver Hummel and Saida Ellen Mayfield and graduated from Mossyrock High School, Mossyrock, Washington 1 March 1936. I registered for college at the University of Washington. Against my better judgment, I also joined the Reserve Officer Training Corps (ROTC).

I needed to find a place to live and heard of a place near the ROTC training center. It had rooms with cooking privileges and cheap so I rented a room. The apartments were in a large two-story building with small partitioned bedrooms upstairs.

Having spent some of my earlier days prior to college I had spent some time in Alaska, loving the adventure and excitement, I returned by steerage to Seward. Having been there previously I was now much wiser about the state and what it required.

This second time in Alaska I went to Talkeetna and stayed

Chapter 1 My Life In Freedom

overnight with my Uncle Ben in his small cabin. Uncle Ike was waiting until "Ross," the Peters Creek Mining Camp boss, sent a message wanting him to come. I walked to Peters Creek and Ross immediately put me to work and I worked the washing plant until September when it was time to return to the UW.

Returning to UW I again needed a place to stay with "board and room" during the school year. I do not recall how I knew of the halibut fisherman and his wife but they wanted me to stay with them so his wife would not be alone during his time fishing for halibut in Alaska.

Once school ended I found what I thought would be a permanent job: laundry, waiting on tables, cleaning house (mopping, sweeping, ironing shirts, etc.) for a lady who rented rooms to men working for an auto agency in Seattle. This lasted for two semesters; then I quit.

I did stay at another house with several students that lived on a share-the-cost basis. I now worked at the Camlin Hotel as an elevator operator and my uniform was furnished. To make ends meet during my time off I would substitute for a fellow that had a car parking operation in Seattle. Also I made sandwiches, sold soft drinks, made milk shakes, banana splits, etc., at a soda fountain near the Farmers Market. All of these odd jobs helped me get through my early years at the university.

Between quarters at UW in March 1940, I hitchhiked from Seattle to Detroit to pick up a Plymouth Coupe I had ordered from the factory. To ensure the best rides and stretch my $15.00 traveling money, I wore my ROTC uniform.

In Mandan, North Dakota I thumbed a ride with Carl Richter, a trucker who was hauling eggs to St. Paul, Minnesota. He gave me strict orders to "hop out quick" when we came to a weigh station as he was loaded to the maximum. He was an entertaining fellow and helped the time and miles go fast.

My food costs – Seattle to Detroit – was $2.50. Hamburgers at 10 cents to 15 cents went a long way. Also one driver bought me lunch and a sack of sandwiches to travel on. I gratefully thanked her for the ride and sack lunch. My hotel in Detroit, as I was delayed two nights before I could pick up the Plymouth, was $4.00!

On Highway 90 in Kansas on my way home, I got stuck in the middle of the road as it was not paved, just sticky "gumbo." A pickup truck pushed me and I got to the next town where I turned south to Highway 50 for Denver. Gasoline was 10 cents to 15 cents a gallon in the Detroit area but increased to 25 cents crossing the desert in Nevada. I refused to pay 25 cents and filled up at the last cheap station, taking my chances to travel to the next cheap station! I lucked out and didn't run out of gas. I used my Standard Oil Credit Card to charge all auto supplies.

After the Kansas "gumbo" I made it easily to Denver and parked in a Standard Station about 2 a.m. and tried to sleep in my seat until the station opened so could "fill her up." I was enroute to Steamboat Springs, Colorado. It was freezing when I left Denver and started up a long hill. I remember the Plymouth would go only 25 miles an hour, no matter how much gas I gave it or what gear I used. Of course, I was driving in high gear. I didn't know Berthoud

Chapter 1 My Life In Freedom

Pass was 11,307 feet high. The black road soon turned white, then white snow heaped many feet higher than my car; this was just the beginning of the mountain passes! I didn't own chains, never had thought of them, or if needed, had the money to buy them.

My strategy to get over the rolling hills between passes was to go slow over the top until I was able to see a clear road with no traffic to the top of the next slope; then I would speed up to 25 or 30 miles per hour to make the next hill top. I counted over 40 autos and trucks stuck in the snow banks and highway equipment was busy pulling them out. I was delayed only once when an auto was crosswise in the road; I waited until he had his chains on and got going. It became so cold on the passes that the heavy snow flurries froze on my heated windshield. I turned off the heat and opened my side window so I could see a little more. The wipers had trouble taking off the freezing snow. The next two passes, Muddy Pass at 8,722 feet and Rabbit Ear at 9,426 feet were no problem to me.

When I arrived in Steamboat Springs I asked about the road to Salvory. The men looked at my bare tires and said, "You can't get there. The road has been closed for the past five months! If you want to wait a couple of months it might be open then. Where did you come from?" "Denver," I said. They didn't believe me so I showed them my trunk – no chains! They then told me that to find my Uncle Charles and Aunt Sylvia Fleming go to Craig, Colorado and then north to Baggs, Wyoming as the men knew the Flemings wintered in Baggs.

I made it to Baggs as it was getting dark and they were really surprised to see me and from where I had come. Another chair was pulled up to their table and I shared their delicious dinner. I met the family that evening: Anna Mae, who was at home, Leonard with his wife Leota, and two children. Sylvia made my bed on their davenport across the room from their coal burning stove. I was exhausted so didn't stay up late.

When I awoke during the night and saw the red fire in the stove I became frightened, but then realized where I was and went back to sleep. I slept right through the family coming through the living room and going out into the barn to take care of the animals. I managed to wake up when they came in from chores and had breakfast with the family.

Aunt Sylvia remembered the small change in my pocket so would not let me go until she had a sack of sandwiches ready for me. We went out to take pictures of my "pride and joy," had hugs all around and I left.

Aunt Sylvia convinced me to go to Rawlins, Wyoming to see her daughter, my cousin Maxine, who was going to college at the University. Maxine found me and we had lunch together. It was so cold and windy that I asked "Max" if it was always this way, and she said, "Most always."

My next stop was Vallejo, California where I visited with my school friend, Jimmy Allison, his sister Ruth, and his mother and stepfather, Fred and Lottie Price. Fred helped me get a tire repaired before I left for Seattle and the University's next quarter.

In June 1940, I again visited the Flemings, but this time went to their homestead on the Little Snake River.

Chapter 1 My Life In Freedom

The road from Baggs was a muddy wagon road; no blacktop, just rounded rocks from the creek to fill deep ruts. They still lived in the original log cabin. I remembered the low ceiling and the semi-dark rooms as there was no electricity – a typical western ranch home. Anna Mae helped me saddle a borrowed horse. I had my foot in the right stirrup and was about to mount when Anna Mae yelled at me to stop and get on the other side, and this horse would buck if I had continued on the "wrong" side. I didn't enjoy the ride; my cheek bottoms ended with the BIG BLISTERS and were padded with two large bandages before we returned to Baggs. There was about 1 to 1-1/2 feet of snow, even this late in the season and lots of mud.

During my last two years I worked at Paramount Film Exchange shipping film to theaters all over Washington.

I joined Lamba Chi Alpha Fraternity but moved out when I had to go into the Army. Since I was working my way through college, I could take only 10 or 12 hours of credits, thus did not have enough credit hours to graduate in 1941 with my classmates.

I did take time out for tennis and other interests. It wasn't all work and studying at UW; I still found time to play.

Early in 1941 my friend Cory introduced me to Evelyn "Nell" Geisler. Nell was a student of Aeronautical Engineering at UW. I was impressed! Our first date was to a dinner dance of university students on St. Patrick's Day. We set our wedding date for September 1941.

Chapter 2
Uncle Sam Calls

I had my four years of ROTC training and on 21 March 1941 I took the Oath as a 2nd Lieutenant (Lt.) in the Infantry, U.S. Army Reserves. I continued Spring and Summer school to earn as many credits as possible for graduation, but was short about 20 hours for graduation.

In mid-July 1941, I received notice to report for active duty on 4 August 1941. I was assigned to the 194th Tank Battalion (Tk. Bn.) for training at Fort Lewis, Washington. (The Air Force base at Fort McCloud, Washington and Fort Lewis, Washington became a Joint Base Lewis-McCloud in 2005.) While on training maneuvers in the Montesano/Satsop area in Grays Harbor, Washington, the Commander received an order to return immediately to Fort Lewis and pack up to go to San Francisco enroute overseas.

Chapter 2 Uncle Sam Calls

I was in a quandary – what to do. Harold Gostigan, also serving in the 194th Tank Battalion (Tk. Bn.) said "Go for it!" He even loaned me $50.00 as I was pretty low on cash as 2nd Lieutenants (Lts.) aren't overpaid. I repaid him my first payday in the Philippines.

Colonel (Col.) Miller allowed me five days' leave to get married, so we set our date for 21 August 1941. The wedding notices had to be corrected by hand and the church date changed. We were married in the University Christian Church which I attended, by Pastor Warren Hastings. Pastor Hastings and his wife had been very good friends to me. I was a very nervous bridegroom and said "I DO" every time Pastor Hastings hesitated between sentences or took a breath. Our relatives and friends muffled their laughter. Vernon Hummel, my cousin, may not remember it, but he was the ring bearer. We had a beautiful reception before we took off for a very short honeymoon.

Nell was an excellent student but when I became a Japanese Prisoner of War (POW) she went to work for Boeing in the wind tunnel testing designs for the B-29 bomber which later helped liberate me from the Japanese.

After our too-short honeymoon, I reluctantly returned to Fort Lewis. For the next week or so I was able to spend a little more time with Nell during her off hours. The officers had a going-away party the weekend before we left for San Francisco and the Presidio. We met other newly-wed officers and their wives. I boarded the train and Nell drove my 1940 Plymouth Coupe to San Francisco where we had another few days together before embarking for an unknown destination.

8 September 1941

At the Presidio we received many shots at the hospital, and then we moved to Angel Island in San Francisco Bay.

In Angel Island we picked up our barracks bag loaded to the top with WARM clothes, camera, film, and loads of miscellaneous things only a neophyte traveler would take; even my Sam Brown belt and chain for the scabbard. We hiked from the barracks to the ferry, then to the ferry to San Francisco, then buses to the pier.

In addition to the 194th Tk. Bn. (500-600 men are in a battalion), there were many other military units with their equipment and personnel, plus unassigned personnel such as officers for the infantry and pilots. There could have been 2,500 men that boarded the USS PRESIDENT COOLIDGE, a cruise ship which had been a luxury ocean liner. It was sunk in October 1942 by land mines in New Hebrides and had been partially converted for a troop ship. This was its first trip as a troop carrier. Nell had been waiting at the pier, but shortly after I arrived we had to kiss goodbye as I wasn't allowed to hold up loading and she had to return to Seattle. As far as I could see from the deck, the dock was swarming with troops to be loaded.

It was long after dark before we sailed. I watched the lights of San Francisco disappear as we passed the Golden Gate Bridge and the ship disappeared in the fog bank that was closing in on the city. As I stood at the railing enveloped in thick fog, I finally realized I was heading into the unknown and would not be with my loved ones.

At the entrance to the Purser's Office we received cabin

and table assignments; we received the early dining time. I was all bug-eyed at the luxury we had: tables with waiters, our cabin was mid-ship from the dining room, first-class food and all you could eat. I sent the menus with beautiful tropical scenes on the cover home to Nell. We had first-run movies at night in the dining room. There was a swimming pool forward for the officers and one aft for the enlisted men. Many hours were spent swimming or just sunning by that pool – until I was burned!

16 August 1941

In Honolulu, Ralph Duby from Seattle and I were fortunate to be "picked up" by the wife of the President of the University of Hawaii. She drove around the island and took us to her friend's home near the Pali for lunch. Her friend was the City Attorney's wife. The coconut trees and many flowering shrubs were all in full bloom; I had never seen such beautiful yards and homes –the tropics appealed to me!

We sailed out of Honolulu that same evening just as the sun set. It was so beautiful. About three days later we became aware of a U.S. destroyer following us. By now we had been told our destination was Manila, Philippine Islands. As I became acquainted with the tanker officers, we would wile away our time with idle gossip, such as: "Isn't it wonderful that Uncle Sam is giving us a free cruise to see the islands and bring us back in one year, plus paying us while we are having fun!"

About half way from San Francisco the normal sea color

changed from greenish to a deep blue and the sun welcomed us to Honolulu.

The second day or so out of Honolulu the porpoises began following our ship. They were fun to watch off the bow as they seemed to either be leading or racing the ship. Farther west we watched flying fish speeding away from the ship's wake and watched the phosphorescent waves. The weather was perfect for over a week, then the sea began to have larger swells and clouds sneaked over the horizon and covered the sky. The rain squalls could come and go, but we swam in the pool with or without the sun as it was always warm.

The farther we went, the rougher the sea became. About the third day after we had the first squalls. I woke up one night as the ship was rolling more and more and appeared to be going more slowly. At breakfast that morning we had to hold on to our dishes or they would slide off the table.

When I went out on deck big drops of rain were "slanting sideways" and the ship was really rolling. The rain on my face felt like bee stings. At times the ship's bow was taking on water. Sometime during the afternoon the rain stopped, but the ocean was very rough.

For some reason an exchange of Navy personnel was being required. The destroyer came alongside a hundred feet or so away, and the COOLIDGE lowered a lifeboat. Once in the water the lifeboat bounced like a big ship. A Navy man was dropped by line into the boat, when the waves stopped. The boat angled its way to the destroyer; it looked like a 4-inch toy as the distance became wider. The destroyer was not only going up and down with waves, it was also rolling

Chapter 2 Uncle Sam Calls

enough to take water on its main deck. No transfer could be completed as the lifeboat would have been crushed. Next a line was set up with a charge to send it to the destroyer. The first and second tries missed, the third time worked and the bosun's chair was attached. The man from our ship made it across in a strong wind, up and down, and back and forth. The Navy man from the destroyer was dunked in the ocean when the destroyer rolled on an unusually big wave, but he made it over. The sailors had a hard time retrieving the boat.

Crowds on both boats gave a high cheer when the two-hour show was completed. Our Navy exchange man said the dunking was not cold, but made him want to shower and get clean clothes. The sea was still very rough at dinnertime and there were many empty chairs in the dining room.

My bunk was still making its dizzy rolls until the next afternoon, but I never missed a meal. Perhaps my ride across the Queen Charlotte Sound seasoned me when I was on my 1936 trip to Alaska and I had spent a considerable time at the rails.

By the following day the storm had blown on east and we were back to sun and fun. What we didn't know was that the ship had gone many miles south to avoid the Japanese Islands' air defenses and submarine lookouts for all U.S. ships heading to the Philippines.

By the 16th of September we began to wonder when we would get to Manila. We were writing letters to be mailed when we arrived, and still enjoying our lovely cruise. About the 23rd we talked to a deck hand and he said it appeared to be low clouds on the horizon; one of the ships' officers came by and told us it was the moisture from the islands and we would be there soon.

The next morning we were cruising through the islands. We didn't know what to expect as only humps of green muffins is all we saw. By evening the humps became coconut trees – millions of trees. My memory was jogged by the trees we had seen in Honolulu. I expected to see Manila any time, but the crooked turns through the islands slowed the ship so it didn't arrive until the next morning. It was our first glimpse of Corregidor and the other small islands.

25 September 1941

The Manila skyline and the docks were not as impressive as San Francisco, but it was more interesting to see: the native people, the horse-drawn callaisas (buggies), and the three-wheel bicycle passenger conveyances.

The 194th tank personnel and our baggage were driven directly to Fort Stotsenberg and to our tent camp next to the parade ground. The officers had one area with two men to a tent. We were issued canvas cots with cotton pads and Government Issue (G.I.) wool blankets and white sheets.

The large kitchen tent was a short distance away; beyond this were the enlisted men's tents. A large area beyond the kitchen was prepared for showers with a nozzle every 6 feet and 6 separate nozzles for bathers; there was a flat board rack to stand on so you were off the ground and the long grass. The water was warm from long, hot sunny days, but on cloudy, rainy days the water was cold and we would take short showers!

Chapter 2 Uncle Sam Calls

The Officer's Club was about three blocks away towards Fort Stotsenberg Headquarters (Hqs.). When off duty in the evenings "Rum & Coke" was the favorite beverage. All drinks were charged and paid monthly. Our club charges were not mailed until we were on alert duty so we had drinks "on the house."

The USS COOLIDGE was unloaded during the time we were getting our camp site set up and we watched them build more permanent buildings to sleep in. The equipment: Tanks, trucks, jeeps, etc., were driven to Fort Stotsenberg before the second week was over.

The next two days were spent by the officers getting acquainted with the post and a visit to the airport at Clark Field only a few blocks away. Here I met my old classmate from the University of Washington. Gary was co-pilot of a B-17 bomber. Clark Field had GOOD tailor shops – all competing to make suntan pants, shirts, and suits of good material. They also had other items such as sun hats with broad brims. I placed an order for several sets of suntan pants and shirts, a white suit of sharkskin material, a pair of white shoes, and a few white shirts to use when off duty to go into Manila and see the city.

I was Platoon Commander (Plt. Com.) of five 14.3 tons light armored tanks and responsible for training the crew. Platoon Lieutenants were in charge. I had the manuals and had to study them, but my studying was by the "light of midnight oil." Training began with the 30 caliber (cal.) machine guns, then 50 cal., and ended up with the 30 cal. rifles in the tanks. Manuals were delivered to each Sergeant

(Sgt.) and the Sgt. taught the crew of each tank. At least four hours a day were spent on dismantling and putting back together the different guns until it could be done blindfolded. I supervised and made checks on each crew before we went on to the next caliber gun. We did not fire any of the weapons as the General would not issue any ammunition because of orders from General (Gen.) MacArthur. It was to be saved until needed!

September went by quickly. Everything was new to us and we enjoyed trading with the Negritoes (small Philippine people who lived in the mountains near Mt. Pinatuba which erupted so violently in 1991). They wanted salt, soap, sugar AND ANY SIZE NAILS and were trading bows and arrows, and some crude knives. They even had made some carrying cases for the bows. We also took the Battalion (Bn.) Scout car loaded with officers to Angeles to a wood carving shop and bought beautiful items. We packed them up and sent them home via the next ship.

The Battalion companies had Harley Davidson motorcycles for messenger use between fighting units and Bn. Hqs. Two or three of us learned how to start them up and ride around the big field next to the tanks. On our next free weekend we drove the motorcycles to the main highway and to various barrios and little villages many miles away from Fort Stotsenberg. I got some good pictures to send home.

The next weekend Col. E. B. Miller called us in and read the riot act to us: "I don't want to see you or hear of you being on those motorcycles again. Only the messengers (Privates–(PVTs) are allowed on them. I need you and you may be

Chapter 2 Uncle Sam Calls

hurt or killed!" Our weekend leave was cancelled.

Going into Manila to go dancing was one diversion.

About five of us attended a dance where we could pick any girl we wanted to dance with — subject to a chaperone's approval, usually the girl's mother. While wearing our uniforms we never had a refusal to dance, but we never could leave the hall with any girl. There was only punch available to drink.

I wore the sharkskin suit once to Manila. The 2nd Lts. and I visited the HiLi games near the Manila Hotel. The HiLi games are of Spanish origin and quite popular in the Philippines. It was played with some kind of contraption strapped to your arm with a holder-like half a coconut shell beyond the end of your fingers for catching a ball about the size of a baseball. You would hit the ball against a wall with it, playing in teams. I enjoyed watching them play.

After the games we went to the Manila Hotel but did not get to the top where Gen. MacArthur had his headquarters. After a lot of walking in the city we hired a Calesa (buggy) and horse to take us sightseeing.

Life was easy during this time at Fort Stotsenberg. Industrious Philippine boys, possibly 12 or 13 years old, made the beds, polished shoes, picked up our laundry and returned it all cleaned and pressed. Our only requirement was to furnish the soap! Their prices were so cheap and their work was so good, we could not refuse. They were honest and watched over us and our belongings.

One weekend Ralph Duby arranged to take an Officer's Scout car and we went to Pagsanjan Falls. It was a beautiful, exciting ride in the chance as the river was running at high water. One of the natives had a load of coconuts on his carabao cart and he cut one of the coconut husks off, made a hole in the coconut, and gave us a taste of coconut milk. We bought some little bananas and enjoyed them for the first time. The mangoes were the biggest hit – they made for sticky fingers, but we loved the taste and it is still my favorite fruit.

About the second week in October gasoline became available for our tanks and vehicles and training was begun. The tanks were new to all the men. The only way to become familiar was to actually work with them. The Gen. would radio to the company Capts. the Capts. would give the orders to the platoon Lts. I was a Plt. Com. and as the orders came to me I would pass them on to my five tanks and their crews to carry out.

At times it was impossible to hear the Capt's. calls; other times the radios were out of order. We usually ended up by using hand signals. Inside the tank were handles to turn the turret by cranking it around 360 degrees; in addition, there were many other knobs on the inside wall for peep holes, etc. When we went over the dry rice terraces it was almost impossible to see the other tanks because of the dust. Breathing was difficult even using my handkerchief over my nose. The sharp drop-offs between the terraces were worse; I was knocked against the walls, bumped my head or hit my back or elbows many times on the tank protrusions.

On the weekend of 20 October 1941, several officers and I drove to Mount Arayat to a swimming pool. It was a lovely swim and we bought coke and candy from the natives.

That night I had the most violent cramps and was sent to the Fort Stotsenberg hospital. It was dysentery and I was very sick for the next two weeks.

The time flew by in October and November with only a few trips to see the islands. I had fun on "Official" business when two of us went on a scouting mission to locate areas to hide our battalion of tanks in case we had to move if there was a war. We checked areas possible to use for parking and bridges were not strong enough to carry tanks. All were marked on our map. We were out two or three days. Upon our return we turned in our maps and were advised we had to "stand by" in case there was an alert. No more fun trips! We visited the Tagaytay, Lake Taal, and Los Bános Lakes.

About the middle of November we were advised that a full alert was expected. About this time the 192nd Tk. Bn. came to Manila and camped next to our area. The 194th had lost Co. B tanks who were sent to Alaska and Co. D was taken from the 192nd and transferred to the 194th. On 25 November I was assigned to Co. D with Altmon as Commander. The Battalion had its last training on a tank trip to Lingayen. The sun was shining and the traffic was heavy after we turned onto the Gulf Road from a good concrete road to a narrow gravel road. The local buses and carabao carts left very little space to pass. When we reached the Village of Lingayen the bus driver parked his bus in the middle of the street. The first platoon of tanks sounded sirens to clear the way; the bus driver just jumped out and watched the tanks come. The tankers drove by and tore off all of one side of the bus; all 52 tanks kept on going – not all missed the side of the bus. The bus driver and the town mayor threatened to sue us! They never did.

We bivouacked about a half mile out of town on a hard sandy beach. My tank was near a beautiful palm tree; the big limbs reached out about 12 feet and just missed the sandy beach by a couple of feet. Here was my first choice to lay my sleeping bag and I spread a big stack of little leaves early for my mattress. A couple of my Lieutenant friends agreed and tossed their bags along side. The sun was setting, the water was warm, the surf was low, and it looked like a perfect place to swim. We promptly shed our sloppy coveralls and shoes and skinny dipped until the sun almost disappeared. When we returned to the chow line Dr. Hickman and Dr. Leo Schneider told us we should not swim without ear plugs as the warm water had live bacteria that would give us ear infections that were very hard to cure! We were lucky — all of us were okay.

After chow we returned to the beach and climbed into our sleeping bags. In a little while my buddies asked if I heard any humming and scratching noises. I put my ear down and listened just above the leaves and I was shocked! Using my flashlight as it was very dark under the low-hanging palm leaves, I discovered about a "million" beetles and nameless bugs under the leaves. We promptly left our "cozy" retreat for a new spot on the smooth sand. The sun rose too early, but we had to get going or miss breakfast. The equipment was already being gassed and being made ready to go back to our home camp, Fort Stotsenberg. The damaged bus was gone and the street quickly cleared as soon as the first tanks were sighted in Lingayen. The little kids and most grownups waved to us and we returned their greetings.

The humidity in the Philippines was really high. We always felt cold and clammy until our bodies dried the sheets and it was cold with TWO wool blankets over us. Our leather shoes would be covered with green mold if they were not dried in the hot sun and cleaned regularly. The barracks were soon ready and were drier with almost no mold.

I always hated Officer of the Day (O.D.) duty. Every few hours, day and night, we had to check on the guards to see that they were awake and nothing was damaged or stolen. This included the barracks, mess area, and all vehicles, including trucks, motorcycles, and tanks. This duty was necessary wherever we were, whether in Fort Stotsenberg or on training duty away from camp.

Jane Geisler, my mother-in-law, through the Eastern Star knew people, who had a plantation on Luzon somewhere near Manila, but when the invitation arrived, I could not go. I was on alert so was very disappointed. I did not even get a chance to write to them why I was unable to accept. We were put on alert to watch for Japanese as it was thought they might make a parachute landing on the Clark Field Airport. I sent all my winter uniforms and some other clothes to Manila for safe storage and my chest was padlocked in the new officer's quarters. It was probably taken by the Filipinos as I never returned to Fort Stotsenberg.

Fort Stotsenberg, during the World War II era, was the location of the Philippine Department's 26th Calvary Regiment (Cal. Reg.), 86th Field Artillery Regiment

(Art. Reg.), and 88th Field Artillery Regiment (Art. Reg.) ; along with the Philippine Division's 23rd and 24th Field Artillery Regiment. Based here also were the 12th Ordinance Company and a platoon of the 24h Quartermaster Regiment.

1 December 1941

We were on full alert. Our job was to protect Clark Field. Our positions were along each side of the two runways that made a big "V" with the Air Corps Hds. and hangers at the head of the "V." My platoon's position was about the middle of the main landing and take-off strip. We stayed here day and night and chow was sent by pickup truck three times a day. We slept on the ground under the shade trees.

7 December 1941

We were finally issued ammunition for the tanks and our side arms. The crews were busy that afternoon loading the 30-mm shells, armor piercing and high explosives, as well as the 30 cal. bullets. When the chow came we still had more to load.

CHAPTER 2 UNCLE SAM CALLS

Chapter 3
WAR

8 December 1941

The next morning we continued to load ammunition. About 11:00 a.m. someone from Headquarters came to our area and told us that Honolulu had been bombed. This was 7 December in Honolulu.

About 12 noon or 11:15 Manila time, as we waited for the chow truck to come, I was talking with some of the Lts. on our side of the defense line. Rice looked up and said there was a big formation of planes coming from the south. I made the comment: "Who said we didn't have a big Air Force out here?"

As we watched the formation changed direction to northwest, I had counted up to 21 bombers when the bombs began hitting the Air Force mess hall and barracks. Before we could move and get behind the ammo cartons we saw the last of the

Chapter 3 WAR

bombs hitting the beginning of the trees where we were and into the landing area. The mess hall and barracks were laid flat and began to burn. The hangers were smoking but were not completely blown down. Holes in the runway would not permit planes to land. Many of the men were able to clear the barracks area, but those in and near the areas bombed were injured or killed.

Our tank crew near the hanger end of the woods had one dead and one with a bad injury. The pickup truck took them to our medics in our camp area. We watched the buildings burn for several minutes as we talked. Some of the men in the tank came out and began loading more ammunition.

Only 5 minutes had gone by and the big formation of bombers was well on their way north to Taiwan. We heard more roaring motors, then another wave of bombers, and then another, almost simultaneously, and machine gun fire were hitting the B-17s parked all around Clark Field. Gary's B-17 plane, my UW friend, was right in front of my tank! The fighters came around the second and third time and his plane was destroyed. The strafing lasted 15 or 20 minutes, but seemed endless. The air base was demolished for all practical purposes. One of the men in one of my tanks loaded the 30 cal. machine gun and fired at the fighters during the second and third passes over Gary's B-17. I could see the tracers going over the Japanese plane but he was unable to damage any enemy planes. We heard the Manila Airport was bombed at the same time.

After our initiation into war, my five tank crews finished loading ammunition. High Command advised Col.

Miller to move the tankers to a nearby road off the airport. There were tall bamboo trees for us to hide under. Before we moved, Gary came to see his B-17; he said it would not fly again. Also he told me his Air Commander had been on the phone all morning trying to get permission to load bombs and fly to Taiwan to bomb the airport from which enemy bombers flew. Each time Gen. MacArthur emphatically told him "NO! The planes are to stay on the ground until I give the order to fly." A POW pilot told me later that Gary did make it to Mindanao where he eventually was ordered to go on to Australia. I never did see him again. We stayed around the tanks watching the leaves fall off the bamboo trees and wondered how bad Manila had been hit with bombs. All day we watched the sky, but no more enemy planes came.

10 December 1941

We moved about half way on the highway to Manila. This was dry rice paddy country and a good place for a parachute landing. Our tanks were parked on a dirt side road off Columpit that had native homes on stilts every 50 to 100 feet. They were built of the typical bamboo strips spaced a quarter to one-half inch. This was for the dirt or any food crumbs to drop through to the chickens below. The house was about seven feet above the ground. A carabao also slept under the house. We arrived in the evening and had time to gas the tanks, have chow, and finished by sunset. The natives were ignored. We were warned that the farmers in this rice growing area were pro-Japanese. Sunset to dark was but a few minutes. Soon afterward we could see fires spaced wide apart across the valley. Some of our men went out and kicked the dry rice paddy dirt on the fire till it went out. After putting out several fires, they looked back and found them burning again. There were two lines of fires which made an "X" and we were in the middle of the "X." No planes showed up that night. We left Columpit barrio the second night and headed for Manila. The "X" fires were burning!

13 December 1941

Before we got to Manila a messenger advised our commander to go on south till we came to a big area with mango trees near a barrio call Muntinlupa. Each of our tanks had a huge mango tree to park under. We were sorry to see no ripe mangos in December (not the season). Here we camped awaiting orders. I sent a telegram to Nell that I was okay. We went through Manila to our new destination. The Japanese were bombing Manila!

I wrote a letter home and sent it to Manila. Later, I wrote another letter and was going to take it myself into Manila. There were 3 of us. An enlisted man was driving, but Capt. Altman and I were going to see what the city looked like and mail our letters. If anyone were to ask us, our "Official Business" was to post company mail and secure supplies.

As we were passing into Pasay (next to a military airport) we noticed traffic leaving town at breakneck speed, but we drove on towards Manila. Then we heard the bombs and saw planes overhead. Away on the road we could see something go flying into the air and then a BOOM! The next bomb sent a shower of dirt into the air and another boom reached us more quickly. Our driver immediately stopped off the road. We jumped out of the jeep into the ditch and some muddy water. Another bomb was coming our way! Fortunately for us, this was the last bomb and our jeep suffered only a couple of bomb fragment hits, but was not disabling. Our ears were ringing and it was very hard to hear for awhile. We returned to the tank bivouac, our mission forgotten and our letters lost.

We loafed around our tank area for a few days. Our only amusement was to watch some of the men walk down the hill and crawl through a wire fence towards a small Nipa (bamboo homes with thatched roofs) shack that had several Philippine women sitting around it. As one would come back, another G.I. would walk down the hill. They all came back with smiles on their faces.

On Christmas Eve we received an urgent message from Gen. MacArthur's Headquarters to "proceed 200 miles to the Agno River Bridge to defend the crossing and delay the Japanese landing at Lingayen Gulf, the area we had scouted earlier. Our orders were to leave our sleeping bags under our mango tree and any other bulky clothes we had. These were to be taken by our rear echelon and brought to our defense area. We never saw our sleeping bags or clothes again.

It was hard to drive the tanks. They "went their own way" and the driver had to constantly correct the steering. A driver was good for about one hour, then the front seat gunner would trade and drive for an hour. This way one person could rest. The radio man, ammo man, and I would take our turns for an hour at the controls. I was happy when my hour was over. We drove all night. In the meantime a sharp lookout was kept for the Japanese scouting plane. The roar of the tank made it impossible to hear the plane, so we just had to keep alert and look around all the time. I remember he came down once to take a shot at us. The turret machine guns made the plane give up as all FIVE of my tanks were shooting at him.

At the Agno River, Co. A, my friend Costigan's group, went upstream for their defense position; 00Co. D, my group, was sent downstream to defend the railroad crossing and the road.

25 December 1941

We stopped under some trees by the road, gassed the tanks, had some sandwiches and coffee, and left as soon as the tanks were gassed. We arrived before dark. Capt. Altman had received orders for us to anchor the west end of the bridge about four miles from the main highway and the Agno River Bridge. The first night we went about 10 miles down the narrow river road and our platoon made camp. Weather was good – hot days and semi-cool nights. We stayed here till next afternoon and had our Christmas lunch. I checked the river up and down for a half mile to make sure there was no place to cross over. The water was deep and there were a few families and some Nipa homes, but very few people were around. I met a young girl along the river with a few dead fish. She wanted to know if they were safe to eat. I checked and told her they were fresh and okay. My guess was that the Japanese had landed big mortar shells in the water and the fish floated away from the concussion. I never saw her again.

26 December 1941

We were ordered to guard the crossing about four miles further south. Capt. Altman ordered my platoon to anchor at the last bridge across the Agno River. There was an auto bridge and a railroad bridge about 100 yards upstream. It was a beautiful place. There were many old palm trees over the entire area between the two bridges and were perfect cover from the air. The tanks were spread out with my tank in the middle of them.

There was a small barrio across the river called Bautista. We never saw any activity there. Before dark about 100 Filipino troops crossed the bridge and took up defensive positions in the tall Sudan grass behind our tanks. The last to cross were the Engineers' demolition crews. They set their explosives to the steel auto bridge and the railroad bridge. Long after dark, maybe about 8:00 p.m., the Filipinos marched away. An hour or so later the engineers set off the auto bridge blast. It woke everyone within miles. The blast sent pieces of steel bracing into the tank nearest the bridge. It cut the leg off the man sleeping on top of the tank. His crew bound his leg as best they could and asked me what to do. I said, "Go to Capt. Altman's HQs under the big mango tree." They did and the man was taken to Battalion Medics. We found out later he was sent back to the United States on the last ship to leave Manila.

I knew that after they blew up the auto bridge, the railroad bridge would follow soon. I advised each of my tank crews to stay in their tanks. About 15 or 20 minutes later it blew with the most ear-shattering boom I have ever heard. For the rest of the night I could hear only if someone shouted in my ear. The explosion sent steel rails into the air in all directions. The palm nearest to the bridge had an almost complete circle of rail wound around its base. The next palm that caught a rail was between two of my tanks, but the rail only bent into a corner-square. In the areas in front and to the rear of my tanks the rails were bent into all sorts of shapes. Some of the palm trees were cut in two. When the blast woke up the other three tankers; they panicked and made a bee-line for Co. HQs. about four miles away. The men in my tank asked to go too, but I refused to leave my post without orders. I foolishly tried to stop the tanks, but would have been run over if I hadn't jumped aside and let them go.

It was a very lonely feeling after the infantry and then the engineers left. The tankers were all that were left manning the crossing at the bridge north of the main highway. It must have been shortly after midnight when I heard a truck roaring along the road across the river. It had its lights on so I "knew" it was a Japanese patrol. I had my ammo man give me an HE 37-mm shell. I shoved it into the gun barrel and aimed it where I estimated it would hit the patrol car. I waited and then heard his roaring back "home" again. As he passed the first opening I made ready. Out he zoomed and I hit the firing trigger. What a shock as the 37-mm roared and pushed me back. The shell was late in taking off and just blew the top off a building across the road. The scout car just drove faster as they heard the explosion. Then we became the object of their search plane as it circled the barrio of Bautista several times early the next morning searching for the gunner that shot at their scouting party.

My crew kept asking to go to Co. HQs but I finally got them to go to sleep. There was no moon and it was pitch black out. It was a scary night, but after the Japanese patrol rushed home with headlights still on bright, I knew they were not likely to cross here. It was a short sleep until daylight. About a half hour after daylight, Capt. Altman came down to the bridge and saw me waiting and we were glad to see each other! He told me there had been shelling at Col. Miller's HQs most of the night, but it was quiet this morning. We went back to his HQs. That was under the big mango tree. The radioman had been trying to reach Bn. HQs all the day before with no luck. We had been out of contact with Bn. Headquarters for over 48 hours! After trying for another hour, Capt. Altman told him to stop trying as the batteries were getting weak.

I was then told to take the armored half-track and contact Capt. Burk's Co. up north along the Agno River to the bridge crossing. His driver started the armored half-track and the Capt. asked who would go along with us. Five Kentucky men volunteered.

27 December 1941

About 1:00 p.m. we took off to find the Co. A tankers. The machine gun was mounted firmly to the right of the driver and the gun barrel was clearing the steel windshield; the driver's view was through a slot in the steel windshield. I was manning the 50 cal. machine gun. Sgt. Causey was standing to my right and watching the road for signs of Co.

Chapter 3 WAR

A tankers; the other men were sitting by the 30 cal. air-cooled machine gun, two on the left and two on the right.

About 4 miles towards Carmen and the bridge crossing we found Sgt. Porwall. He had heard us coming and met us on the road. He told us there had been heavy shelling at Carmen, but it was quiet now. Lt. Hart's platoon was about a mile up the road. We continued on and one of his men met us. I asked for Lt. Hart, but they said he was too afraid to leave his tank. This was the last tanker we contacted, and with a light pat on his back, I signaled the driver to continue on. The machinery and/or gunfire was too noisy for verbal commands. We had driven about 2 miles when we came to the Nips' house where I had stopped 2 days ago. As I recognized the house, a Japanese machine gunner made diagonal passes, starting low to high, at the half-track. I could see every 4th tracer shell burst go by my head like angry bees. A tracer shell is just like a regular bullet, but has silver paint – or something – so the trajectory can be traced. I had the 50 cal. gun aimed under the porch where the bullets were coming from. After 25 or 30 rounds were fired, my gun jammed. The second firing from the Nipa house shot up the half-track's radiator and splashed shells across the windshield. The steel fragments hit me in the chest and face; another shell ricocheted on the edge of the windshield and hit me in the neck. The same burst also hit Sgt. Causey beside me. The energy in these little shells (27 mm) surprised me, knocking me flat on my back onto the flat steel floor. Sgt. Causey fell halfway on me and onto the steel floor. He had been hit in the neck also and couldn't talk or move.

I got up off the floor of the half-track and tried to tell the driver (with foot signals that did not work) to turn around in the middle of the road. He just kept going. I told him again to turn around. I had to hit him on the head with my fist to get his attention and he finally turned around. I think he was "frozen" on the steering wheel. By this time we had gone 300 to 400 feet past the enemy. Now we had to go back past the Japanese gunners. I tried to get the 30 cal. machine gunners to fire and threw some hand grenades. One of them fired the 30 cal. machine gun into the building and under the porch, but no fire was returned. The other men squatted down behind the steel siding. One of the gunners put a big bandage on Sgt. Causey's neck and laid him flat on the floor. I tried to put a big bandage on my wound but had to have help to get it tight. It wasn't tight enough and I ended up with a shoe full of blood and pants soaked on the left side and back.

The armored scout car made it back about three-quarters of a mile before the motor froze due to heat and lack of water. I got the uninjured men to head back towards Co. HQs for Capt. Altman. I started them out in infantry style of an alternate man on each side of the road and well spaced so the enemy could not get them all at once if they met another gunner. Before they were out of sight I could see they were bunched again; they did make good time as Capt. Altman soon returned in a tank. Two squads of tanks from Co. A followed him, except for Lt. Hart and his tank; no one could get him to move. (He did not make it home.) He hitched onto the half-track and towed us back to his HQs.

Chapter 3 WAR

Back at Co. HQs Capt. Altman – the only one with a map – led 15 or 16 tanks and a disabled armored half-track across country to find the main highway south. On the way we picked up 30 or 40 Filipino troops. A few still had their guns. They climbed onto the tanks and the half-track. The column had gone about two miles when we passed a barrio where there was a lot of firing at the tanks. Our Filipino foot troops all took off as the first gun fired and we never saw them again.

I had lost so much blood I was getting helpless fast. It seemed like forever before we were on the main highway south. Fortunately the Japanese had not traveled this far south. It was an easy ride until we met a blasted concrete bridge and a deep river. My sergeant helped me to the ground, and then he dashed out and located two long bamboo poles and fastened them together. I saw Capt. Altman go to the river and then called "Okay" to come across. The troops rushed out. I asked my sergeant to pass the word to disable all tanks. My sergeant dismantled the back plates and firing pins on all our guns and threw the distributor into the water. So did the next tank crew, but I doubt if any more vehicles were disabled. With Capt. Altman's help one of the tank's crew aided Sgt. Causey across the river. Capt. Altman came back, and helped one of my crew get me across. On the way, my "musette" bag with my camera, etc. was dropped into the river. One less thing to carry! It hurt me to see one of tanks and an armored car abandoned. Later I found out there was a shallow crossing a half mile upstream. What a waste!

Fortunately there was a small barrio near the bridge.

One of our men asked the Filipinos for a car; there was a Chevy flat-bed truck. And it had gasoline! I was cramped into the front seat with three others with the Capt. holding me to keep my head from falling onto my chest. I don't know how Sgt. Causey survived the ride or how so many men found a place to hang on, but no one was left behind. About an hour later we arrived at the road block made by the 194th tankers. Sgt. Causey was given immediate first aid and sent to Manila for further treatment. (He made the last boat out to the U.S.) Dr. Hickman and Dr. Leo Schneider gave me bandages, a sleeping pill, and put me on a stretcher to get some sleep. I was then taken to San Fernando Hospital and put to bed.

Chapter 3 WAR

Chapter 4
BATAAN

29 December 1941

Another ambulance took me to Hospital #2 in Limay on the Bataan Peninsula. There had been heavy fighting and shelling in Bataan. Lt. Petrie of Co. C, 194th Tk. Bn. was shot 3 January 1942 on the front line. Doctors fixed the bullet hole in his stomach and he was put in my room. He died 9 January.

4 January 1942

My appointment with the surgeons was this date. I lay down on a large box and made myself as comfortable as possible. The doctor put a block of wood under my head and padded it with a towel. He then carefully poked around and took some steel out of my eye. He was about to check for more in my face when the siren went off. We could hear the airplane motor rev up so we stepped outside the white sheet that served as a door to the hospital. The plane was diving on some Philippino troops marching under a big mango tree on the gravel road about 200 feet from our hospital. I don't understand the stupid commander of the company; they never tried to take cover in the low brush along the road. The small bomb dropped by the scouting plane (we nicknamed it "Washing Machine Charlie") made a direct hit into the middle of the company and made mince meat of many. The plane flew away; it probably had only the one bomb.

The male nurses and a few able-bodied men ran out and picked up the injured and ran with them to the makeshift operating room. I came back and sat down on my *operating table*, but the doctor left me waiting and dashed over to the other side of the room divider sheet. I could hear them talking: "Tighten the tourniquet on his leg; now give me the big saw; a little more pain killer, he's still feeling it; bring the tub over here; it's a better place and I don't have to hit anyone." Then I heard a big thump into the tub. The second patient was on another table in the same room with a crew of doctors working. Again, I saw a stub of an arm with a shattered hand going through the air; the opening between the two operating areas was open about three feet and the injured were also waiting in the room I was in. The doctor saw me and told me he was too busy and to "Get out. We are swamped with seriously injured men who need immediate aid." By then the tub was getting more and more parts of bodies and I was getting sick to my stomach. I was more than happy to get out! Everyone was working at a feverish pace —- even the ward they told me to go to was also used.

7 January 1942

As more and more casualties kept arriving, the doctor finally gave up and told me they didn't have time for me and I could go back to my unit. The medics put a clean bandage on my neck; they had not removed the bullet, and I hitched a ride back to Co. D. I was still very weak from loss of blood. Col. Miller received the remaining 192nd Bn. tanks and had fire power again, but there were no more Co. D tanks, so I was no longer a tank Lt. and became Capt. Altman's Aide.

9 January 1942

Bn. Hqs. and Companies C and D moved a few miles closer to the front line along Pilar-Bagac Road. This was the two-lane highway to the west side of the Peninsula and Subic Bay. Co. D was made the "chow maker" by Col. Miller for the time we were here. Capt. Altman designated me the Officer in Charge. Co. D furnished the rations – delivered by Supply Issue from rear echelon supply. By the second day we did not have enough to feed both Companies C and D and HQ Officers.

I appointed myself chief carabao rustler. With a couple of the kitchen help we walked across the road to a big field and attempted to lasso a fat carabao for dinner. We could get no closer than 50 feet. Two Filipinos came along and offered their help. We pointed out the one we wanted; he walked over, put a rope over the neck, and led it out of the pasture. We took the rope and attempted to go but the carabao started to go back to the pasture. We called the Filipino and he agreed to take it to our camp about a half mile away.

Chapter 4 BATAAN

He tied it to a big mango tree. I got my 45 caliber pistol; while the others stood back, I fired between the eyes of the "beast" which didn't faze it. Another officer got a rifle and took a shot for the heart. The carabao gave a big pull to the rear, broke the rope, and headed for the kitchen truck area. It stopped and looked at us. It was given another shot behind a shoulder and went down. I started to take the skin off so we could cut it into pieces. I soon turned the job over to the two Filipinos who did a fast job. For their efforts, I gave them the hide and the bones, including the head. They also wanted money, so I gave them an IOU on the Government of the United States. This was satisfactory to them.

We had tiny steaks that night, then stew and soup. Two hundred men made the carabao disappear fast. Capt. Altman gave me "hell" for giving away the bones. So much for an amateur kitchen manager!

Bataan is a 30-mile long peninsula about 3 miles north of the Island of Corregidor and is located about 26 miles west across the bay from Manila. The road to Bataan was narrow and dusty gravel. There were huge trees in the midst of the mountains and the jungle, with big vines going from the high tree limbs down to the road. The little family houses here were made of woven bamboo sheets for the floor and sides and a Nipa or rice straw roof. The houses usually were raised above the ground since there were heavy rains during the monsoon season. The big coconut trees were plentiful and beautiful. The villages where the tankers were on watch against the Japanese invasion were situated in the big coconut tree areas and usually had a concrete fountain with a walking area around it. The artisan wall had a good stream of water. The area under the coconut palms was clear with small leaves on the ground. This was a good shady place to be as it had a nice breeze. The fountain was the village work area for laundry and gossip time for the mothers. Villages that didn't have a spring usually had a stream they could pipe into their central area and a concrete fountain for continuous water. A bonus was that some families were still living here and some could speak English. When you looked out to the bay, the water was a continuous lapping on the shore – beautiful. The natives were fishermen or had rice paddies on the inland side of the road.

12 January 1942

Food is scarce and so Quartermaster delivered almost nothing! I found one of the same Filipinos and we had another carabao for a few days. Again, I signed an IOW from Uncle Sam. The next day there were no more carabao; they had been rounded up by the Quartermaster for the hospitals and front line troops.

15 January 1942

Below is Gen. MacArthur's speech as I had it recorded in my diary while I was in the Zentsuji Prisoner of War Camp in Japan. Gen. MacArthur delivered it from his Headquarters on Corregidor.

Chapter 4 BATAAN

HEADQUARTERS
UNITED STATES ARMY FORCES
IN THE FAR EAST
FORT MILLS, P.I.
Jan. 18, 1942
SUBJECT: MESSAGE FROM GEN. MacARTHUR
TO: ALL UNIT COMMANDERS

The following message from General MacArthur will be read and explained to all troops. Every company commander is charged with the personal delivery of this message. Each headquarters will follow-up to insure reception by every company or similar unit.

"Help is on the way from the United States. Thousands of troops and hundreds of planes are being dispatched. The exact time of arrival of reinforcements is unknown as they will have to fight their way through Japanese attempts against them. It is imperative that our troops hold until these reinforcements arrive.

No further retreat is possible. We have more troops in Bataan than the Japanese have thrown against us; our supplies are ample; a determined defense will defeat the enemy's attack.

It is now a question of courage and of determination. Men who run will merely be destroyed but men who fight will save themselves and their country.

I call upon every soldier in Bataan to fight in his assigned position, resisting every attack. This is the only road to salvation. If we fight we will win; if we retreat we will be destroyed.

MacArthur"
By command of Gen. MacArthur
(Signed) Carl H. Seals
Carl H. Seals, Col. AGLA,
Adjutant General
"Copy"

18 January 1942

A battery of 155's were bombed at Orien cutoff. A "155" is a cannon firing a big 6-inch shell. Casualties were unknown and damage minimal as was shown later.

22 January 1942

Across the road from our bivouac some supply trucks were bombed on a cutoff from our HQ. One truck loaded with food for front line troops was destroyed. The Japanese had freedom of the sky. At first our 4 or 5 P-40s could keep the scouting planes away, but their Zeros were out-shooting the P-40s because they were superior in mobility and in number. Our P-40s were mainly used for scouting Japanese activity on the ground. The Abucay defense line originally established 3 January was very active, but could not be held.

26 January 1942

The 194th Tk. Bn. moved their tanks to support the withdrawal of the front-line Infantry and light artillery to a new defense line farther down the peninsula. after the line was ready, the tanks moved south of the line into a mango grove approximately ½ mile from the main east side road. (We still had no ripe mangoes.) Co. A provided enough tanks to give Co. D a full platoon of tanks as Capt. Altman had lost tanks on the Agno River retreat. The 194th and 192nd Tn. Bns. were combined and sent along the east coast to stop a Japanese landing by night behind the front line. The 194th supplied their units with food from the Co. D kitchen, but the food supply was disappearing fast.

1 February 1942

The Japanese made a landing behind our lines at Cabcabin, a Filipino village, and burned it; they went back to their lines before daylight. Hospital #1 at Lemay was hit by bombs and evacuated. The Japanese were temporarily stopped and there was a lull in the fighting.

There was a general food shortage. The jungle was searched for bananas, palm cabbages, or other food items. From our bivouac, Dr. Hickman and I scouted the central area of small, steep hills for anything edible. Nothing was found. I think some 3 to 4,000 civilians probably had been there long before us. Later, I bought a few green bananas from natives near the main road south on the highway to Mariveles, the last village on the tip of the peninsula. Food rations were cut in half again the first of the month.

15 February 1942

The Japanese did not make any more assaults on our line and there was a lull. During this time we dug fox holes in the bivouac area. One ambitious group of men installed a 50-cal. machine gun on a little hill to the west of our camp.

They dug it in so the Japanese scouting plane could not easily shoot them. Every morning, within minutes of a time schedule, "Washing Machine Charlie" made his run down the peninsula. He flew so low that it was a perfect time to shoot him down. The first time the gun put a few holes into his wings, he zoomed up immediately and headed for home in a wobbly line. From then on he avoided our gun and it was eventually returned to its original place.

During this time we did many things, such as taking a bar of soap and going to the river just north of our bivouac. It was a steep slope down to the river, about 400 feet down. The small river was clear and warm. We swam and washed our sweat-stiff coveralls, socks, and hung them on the big, hot rocks to dry. Weather was cool early in the morning but could get up to 98 degrees during the day. The climb out of the river ravine was a real sweaty job and the coveralls were soaked again, but we didn't care as they were clean and we would be dry for a few minutes just standing or sitting still in the sun.

Except along the shore of Manila Bay, if there was a breeze, mosquitoes were thick on Bataan. They carried malaria and it was "take your Quinine regularly or suffer." By the 1st of March many were incapacitated with malaria fever. Quinine pills were gone and only the powder was available. Many men took the powder into their hand and when Dr. Schneider wasn't looking, they tossed it. He did make a soft Quinine pill later, but most of the troops would not listen to the doctor's advice. By the middle of March there was no Quinine available. A substitute was issued once, and then

Chapter 4 BATAAN

it was also gone.

10 March 1942

During the lull in fighting Gen. Douglas MacArthur and his staff came from Corregidor and drove to Mariveles to see the front lines. The Japanese were waiting for reinforcements from China.

This poem is also from my diary:

COURAGEOUS CORREGIDOR MAC

From out of his hole, four stories below, Crept courageous Corregidor Mac

With a 155 to keep him alive, and a howitzer strapped on his back.

I will ride thru Bataan. As fast as I can, Rest assured I am practically back.

While I'm there, I will declare, that supplies are well on their way,

I ordered carabao steak, and rice patty cakes to keep your hunger away,

I will tell Franklin D. of all that I see, And a little more to boot,

Of skies being black when our bombers attack and any more "bull" I can shoot!

Get my Cris Craft ready,

For I'm a bit unsteady; I've had a hard day on the line,

I must hurry back to my underground shack. Brother Quezon is anxious to dine!

Author Unknown

20 March 1942

There is still not much action on the front lines. We watched the scouting planes on their daily runs. One time there was a lot of American anti-aircraft firing around the scouting plane and we saw the plane make a couple of fast maneuvers and fly away. We were surprised to hear heavy rain noise from the bamboo trees – it was the shrapnel from the anti-aircraft shells coming down. We quickly grabbed our metal helmets, but it was too late. We were lucky, no casualties; just a lot of ringing in our ears.

Another time four officers, including me, took the old Chevy, which was made into a flatbed truck, for a drive towards Mariveles at the tip of the peninsula. It was too far, so we turned back to our bivouac area. We were just crossing a P-40 dirt airport when the Japanese scout plane saw us and started diving and shooting at us. One of us saw and heard the noise and yelled to stop. We jumped fast and ran back about 30 feet to a low ditch along the side of the runway. I looked up and saw two bombs coming down! I stopped looking and stretched out into the ditch and put my head as close into the dirt as possible. The first bomb hit about 40 feet away and the shrapnel cut the top off the grass and off some little bushes. The second bomb landed about 100 feet away. No one was hit. The Chevy truck took some shrapnel but was usable.

25 March 1942

Food is very scarce and we are down to one-quarter rations. Everyone is hungry and losing weight. Again we went into the jungle to find anything edible. The Philippinos had showed us some trees that had a "cabbage-like" top that we used for green salad and sometimes cut it up for soup. Coconuts were welcome, but not obtainable – who could climb those high coconut palms? Also the native Army troops as well as the civilians were starving and ate anything they found. During our carabao eating days we ran into a small six-foot lizard (iguana) in a small creek near our camp which the natives asked us to shoot. I'm sure it ended up in their cooking pot. We remembered all this when we were hunting for food to help our skinning rations.

Dr. Hickman's and Dr. Schneider's hospital for the Bn. was located under some tall brush and some young overhanging bamboo about 20 feet tall. About 15 or 20 men who had malaria and other illnesses were lying on blankets on the ground. Nearby two foxholes were semi-hidden under some shoulder-high brush. Many more foxholes were scattered among more bamboo away from the mango grove under which our tanks were concealed.

March 1942 was fairly quiet until the last week, when activity picked up with more reconnaissance and air activity. Also, the heavy artillery of the Japanese began location range firing where I happened to be. I was visiting my old Colonel teacher from UW. He must have been 60 or more; at least he looked it. The 205 mortars sent a lone shell into our area. In a few minutes another shell came screaming in; this one landed closer to the highway road on the Manila side and nearer to our foxhole. It was real scary, even to the Colonel. The shrapnel and rocks whistled just over our heads and cut off the brush. Another shell landed closer to the highway, and the shelling continued until they hit close to a big mango tree which had the road on both sides of it. The shelling stopped. We later heard it was to protect a landing from Manila Bay to take the peninsula. No landing was made.

1 April 1942

Japanese air activity increased on the front lines. Big Japanese bombers hit the First Corps' front lines on the east side of Manila Bay. In the afternoon the heavy bombers also hit the Second Corps on the west. Smaller bombers hit the Quartermaster food dump, the main hospital, a small ordinance depot, and the artillery spotter on Mount Sumat.

The bombing was watched most of the day from a hill behind our bivouac. Front line bombing was from daylight to dark. After dark the smaller planes dropped bombs off and on just to keep the front lines from reorganizing. The scout planes watched for supply trucks heading to the front line and would bomb them. The front lines didn't get food, water, or any new ammunition supplies for over three days. There was a constant dust storm over the front lines.

5 April 1942

The 194th Tn. Co. C was sent to the front to cover any breakthrough in the First Corps. Co. D was sent to reinforce Co. C at Trail Road No. 2-10-J. The trail roads were only car or truck width, cut between tall and small trees over the main hills to the coast road. This was the dry season and the tanks chewed up the brush stubs and the dirt to brown powder was many inches thick. The dust was blinding.

The front was busy with Japanese coming through the lines everywhere. The tanks did a good job where they could drive, but there were too many places with small to deep ravines and had to be bypassed. One of the tanks got too near the edge of the road and rolled over into a 20-foot deep ravine before it stopped. The crew, after trying hard to move the tank, got out into the other tanks. They were shaken up, but not injured. Brig. Gen. Weaver, Provisional Tank Group, United States Army in the Far East (USAFFE) insisted the tank wrecker pull out the tank and a full day was spent in a futile effort to rescue the tank. The Japanese kept circling the area and were taking "pot shots" every chance they had. Japanese planes began dropping their bombs; they made the fighting one hell of a situation. By early afternoon, they had to give up and the tankers headed back out. The foot troops had retreated to their next line by night. The front line, consisting mainly of Philippino troops, was told to retreat to the next line of resistance. It was impossible to maintain any defense. The troops were hungry, thirsty, and very tired trying to keep the very superior numbers of Japanese from taking the area. The Japanese were bombing very heavily, plus they were strafing and bombing where the heavy dust marked the retreat from the front line.

6 April 1942

The tanks came back just as the sun was ready to go down, coming in 5 to 10 minutes apart, and parked under the big mango trees. They had held a short area of the front and stopped dozens of Japanese Infantry as the Japanese came through a cornfield and another area where there was a clearing. The Japanese Infantry paid a heavy price where our tanks could see them. The Japanese had given the tanks a wide berth as the tanks were bullet proof against rifle fire. "Washing Machine Charlie," loaded with small bombs, followed the column of dust made by our tanks, dropping the bombs in the middle of the mango trees, and the last bomb near the edge of the trees. This bomb hit our half-ton pickup loaded with 30 and 50 cal. shells. The boxes of shells ignited sending the bullets going one direction and the shell casings the other. Everyone was in their foxholes, plus any others from the sickbay under the bamboo shelter. One area of foxholes had dirt thrown over them from the half-ton truck fireworks which lasted for nearly an hour. The entire truck, tires all burned; the gas tank sent a big ball of flame when it exploded. The heavy dust was hard to breathe; it covered our coveralls in big splotches where we had perspired. Our evening meal, can't remember what, was very skimpy. We did have water in our five-gallon cans on the kitchen truck; a little was allowed to wash our faces, but most was used for drinking.

7 April 1942

The General of the Provisional Tank Group ordered the 194th tanks to move south again and off the main road where we hid under big trees. We were on a hill that leads to a trail road connecting to the front lines. The air was busy with Japanese planes over Corregidor dropping lots of bombs as

CHAPTER 4 BATAAN

they were trying to keep Corregidor's artillery from firing on the Japanese advance into Bataan. The smaller planes were busy dropping bombs and strafing.

We were all very tired and hungry. Our whole line of defense was enroute to our rear. Vehicle traffic on the road past our bivouac was in long lines of vehicles with soldiers hanging on everywhere as best they could; they were dirty and slumped over with exhaustion. The bombing and shelling went on all night.

8 April 1942

Traffic was heavy on the main road to Mariveles. The day was hot, humid, and very little shade; water was getting very low. Air traffic was busy as usual, but traffic from the front trail road was slow; then it would speed up and be very heavy for an hour or more. About 3 or 4 p.m. Col. Miller received word that we were to meet at KM-168-1/2-1 turn toward the bay, and park our vehicles. The word was passed down to all on the road that a jeep with Gen. King and his staff was driving north to surrender to the Japanese command.

> STRANDED IN BATAAN
> They sent us to the Philippines; we thought it a vacation,
> This visit to the land of dreams
> Proved our ruination.
> No sooner had we landed,
> That the Japanese came in to meet us,
> With planes and bombs and tanks, and guns,
> They all came down to greet us.

They chased us from Fort Stotsenberg,
Down to Legaspi Bay
Back up to Lingayen Gulf,
Then down to Bataan to stay.
So here we sit beside the shore,
Just waiting for our aid,
And listening to the radio,
Tell how much the U.S. has made.

This poem was written by an unknown author but described our feelings so well. I was able to have it recorded in my diary – which I kept in Zentsuji POW camp.

By the time we got our vehicles and tanks on the Mariveles main road it was time for the sun to set. The road was crowded and moved in spurts. We came to a curve in the road where a big truck was about four feet into the road and blocking traffic. Two Filipinos were trying to get it out of a deep ditch into which they had accidentally backed and could not get out. We waited about 15 minutes and I got out of my tank to see what the trouble was. Col. Miller was in his tank 3 or 4 vehicles ahead, but no one had gotten out to see what the trouble was or to help them. I told them to back further down into the ditch and not to block the traffic; also told them to grab the first vehicle they could and ride. The line began to move again. About this time a plane came over and dropped two bombs on the attractive target traffic. It misjudged the timing and hit a camouflaged ammunition dump about 100 feet off the road. The noise was deafening with the shells going by at a high speed, making a sizzling sound. The small arms ammunition was setting off other larger ammo which, in turn, was setting off the bigger and bigger shells. A huge fire flashed into the sky with a big boom which really lit up the area. Traffic did not linger at this point as it was dangerous; the bullets would go off and hit vehicles in their paths and the empty shells would go sailing through the air.

About midnight most our group was off the road and resting. The big trees made a perfect place to hide. The ammo dump was still burning brightly and the "booms" could be heard five miles away. Now we just sat around talking and speculating what was going to happen next. All kinds of thoughts were expressed as from what we had heard, anything could happen, even to being a Prisoner of War (POW).

9 April 1942

Gen. King surrendered Bataan to the Japanese.

Chapter 5
BATAAN DEATH MARCH

The Bataan Death March began 9 April 1942. It was a forcible transfer by the Imperial Japanese Army of approximately 140,000 Filipino and American prisoners of war after a three-month Battle of Bataan. It is estimated about 2,500 to 10,000 Filipino and 100-650 American prisoners died before they reached Camp O'Donnell who got its name from a family of early Spanish settlers in the late 1800's.

(Author's Note): When I was a youth in my history class either we were told or imagined that the death march was over many, many miles, when in fact, it was about five to eight miles from Bataan. According to the Internet it was approximately 80 miles from beginning to end; however, some of this mileage includes when the prisoners were loaded into box trains, generally so stuffed with human beings that there was standing room only with no ventilation in tropical heat.

Chapter 5 BATAAN DEATH MARCH

Pity the poor individual that had to eliminate urine or feces!

The prisoners suffered from starvation, many illnesses, and physical abuse and if one of the prisoners needed assistance from one of the other prisoners, it was offered, but all of them were suffering in one manner or another. Many were bayoneted for lagging behind. Some were even bayoneted just because …

Chapter 6
Corregidor

<u>*10 April 1942*</u>

About 1:00 a.m. (Philippine time) Lt. Al Herold, also from the 194th Tn. Bn. and I walked around our area and down to the bay where a small creek came off the hill into the bay. We went back to our bivouac where Al had an empty 5-gallon water can and I got one of our empty cans to go with him. Al's Sgt. Fergeson, and my Sgt. Aaron Hopper, agreed to go and took water cans. Once we arrived at the creek's entrance into the bay, Herbold and I decided we could swim to Corregidor as it looked so close. Our sergeants opted to go with us. All this time Corregidor was lobbing big mortar rounds over our heads toward the front lines. The noise, if you can imagine it, made the sound of a box car tumbling about 100 feet over our heads. Actually, the rounds were a few miles away. Lt. Herold and Sgt. Fergeson started first. Sgt. Hopper and I sat down and took our shoes and coveralls off. I tied my pistol, coveralls and shoes to the empty water can and tied it to my back; Sgt. Hopper tied his water can

Chapter 6 Corregidor

to his back also and we started swimming in just our shorts. Lt. Herbold and his sergeant must have been a long way ahead of us as we could not find them. It was dark, no moon with only stars for light. We kept on swimming with no regard for sharks or barracuda; we found out later that the bombing and shelling had driven the sharks and barracuda out of the bay.

Towards early morning we discovered we had drifted toward Manila. The longer we swam the farther the tide began taking us to the south end of the island. In a little while a water tender boat, VAGA, commanded by Warrant Officer (W.O.) Downey, U.S. Navy, picked us up. He swung his "45" around as though he couldn't decide if we were spies for the Japanese, or what. We soon realized he was drunk as the more he talked the more slurred his words were. He finally calmed down and decided to go towards Bataan and shell the Japanese. He ordered his crew to fire his 3-inch shells toward the east side of the peninsula. The only thing he could possibly have done was to hit some of the retreating troops, or possibly some Japanese. He turned around and headed south again for the north dock of Corregidor. He dropped anchor about 100 yards or so off the dock. It was becoming light by then. A small Japanese reconnaissance plane flew over and dropped two small bombs; one landed to the rear of the boat and the second just off the side of the boat. I was sitting by the cabin, water, and mud splashed all over me and the cabin. The boat's crew kept the plane up high with their 50-cal. machine guns. In spite of the machine guns, the plane made another dive at the boat, missed it, and flew north for more bombs. After the Japanese plane left, the boat was transferred to south dock.

I picked up my "45," put on my wet shoes, and we went ashore on the Navy side. My coveralls were not completely dry, but that is all I had; Sgt. Hopper fared the same as I. We were escorted ashore by W.O. Downey and he reported to his superior. We, Sgt. Hopper and I, were sent over to the Army side in Malinta Tunnel to report to Col. Bowler for duty. I don't know where Sgt. Hopper was assigned as I never saw him again. I was assigned to the 59th Military Police (MP) Co. with Capt. Benson commanding.

My duties were to take a platoon and see that they were available to man the machine guns at the north and south ends of the tunnel and the west end of the hospital. I met the Sergeant reporting to me and some of the men. We inspected each of the three locations and they were "ready to go." It was agreed that we meet at the north end of the tunnel each evening before dark or if the island was attacked. This worked if there were no shells coming into the island. The men were allowed into the tunnel if the shells were hitting tunnel areas. Everything went okay for a few days, but it wasn't long before the guns were not manned as shells were coming too close to the gun locations. The gun sites were soon covered with rock debris.

Corregidor itself is 3-1/2 miles long and about 2 miles wide at the widest point; from the air it looks like a tadpole. The U.S. Navy had built a search-light on its highest point, which had three different elevations: topside, middle-side, and bottom-side. Bottom-side was the docks. It is a labyrinth of

Chapter 6 Corregidor

tunnels bored into solid rock and was virtually bomb proof.

The largest tunnel was Malinta Tunnel, running from one side of 400 foot-high Malinta Hill to the other side. Branching off the 30-foot-high main tunnel were 25 lateral tunnels, each being about 150 feet long. An underground hospital was housed in another tunnel system and the Navy and Quartermaster Corps occupied still another subterranean space.

My bunk area was located at the end of the 4th tunnel, from the east entrance. This 150-foot tunnel had bunks on both sides with steel cots 2 bunks high. Cotton mattresses softened the springs a bit. By the time I arrived the bunks were doing double duty, always had a shift sleeping. At the east end was a connecting tunnel about 75 feet long with a ceiling about 2 to 3 feet high and full of jagged rocks from when the Navy blasted the tunnel on the south side of Corregidor. It was here that I slept. At first I didn't have any blankets or extra clothing to build up between me and the sharply-pointed rocks where I lay down. When I received blankets, I used them and any clothes I wasn't wearing. It was not safe to get up fast as I could receive a "bloody" knot in my head. The tunnels in Corregidor were blasted out of solid rock and my private bedroom was no exception – there was about 200 feet of rock in my ceiling. It was much safer than an outside foxhole, but it was hot with very poor circulation. There was lots of cigarette smoke even though it was a "no smoking" area. Heat rash was also a problem. At the Navy end of the unfinished tunnel was a room filled with cartons of canned food. The only time I raided it was shortly before surrender when I took two big cans of unlabeled food. They turned out to be peach halves which three of us enjoyed before leaving the tunnel at surrender.

11 April 1942

The surrender of Bataan did not slow the Japanese bombing all the island fortresses: Corregidor, Fort Frank, Fort Hughes, and Fort Drum. The bombs blew down many trees and exposed many hidden artillery sites. Tons of bombs were dropped every day, with many falling on the Malinta Tunnel hill as well as suspected artillery sites. The heavy bombs made the old "Rock" shake. I sometimes wondered if the tunnel roof was going to fall on me; it was not a happy thought with which to go to sleep. I could only ask God to keep me alive.

As soon as the Japanese Army got to Mariveles their troops began rounding up the American and Philippino troops and sending them on the road to San Fernando. The troops north of Mariveles were held only long enough to have a certain number and then escorted north. During this time Japanese artillery was headed south with heavily laden ammunition trucks following artillery. The biggest guns and the largest (240-millimeter (mm) howitzers were set up for action and were all focused on Corregidor. Now they made the American and Philippino prisoners sit around the batteries of guns and howitzers so the Americans could not fire from Corregidor without killing their own troops. The hostages were held several days as new prisoners arrived; they were placed in front of Japanese guns and the first group was marched away to prison camp. Our officers, with their binoculars, could

Chapter 6 Corregidor

see the Japanese doing this to our captured men and the decision was made not to fire on the Japanese position from Corregidor. Hundreds of POW's lives were saved to make the bloody Bataan Death March to San Fernando, then ride to Capas in hot steel, jammed tight and locked steel rail cars. From Capaz they again marched to Camp O'Donnell.

Camp O'Donnell was a facility of the United States Air Force in Capas, Tarlac, the Philippines. Before the facility was transferred to the Air Force, it was originally a Philippine Army post and later a United States Army facility. It is now a camp of the Armed Forces of the Philippines. During the Japanese occupation of the Philippines during World War II, it was the final stop of the Bataan Death March and was used as an internment camp for Filipino and American prisoners of war. Around 20,000 Filipinos and 1,600 Americans died there. It was liberated on 30 January 1945. It is presently maintained as a shrine built and is maintained by the Philippine government as a memorial for those who died there.

While inspecting the 30-cal. guns, my sergeant and I were caught out in the open. I didn't hesitate to crawl into a small wing of concrete on the hospital side entry under Malinta Tunnel. The Japanese's big guns were hitting higher up the hill. I got out half an hour later when they quit firing. Artillery shells are pretty bad and I prayed to God again as I was really scared. Shrapnel and rocks were coming off the Rock a few feet from our refuge.

This brings up another subject: FOOD! There was less food served here than our quarter ration would have been in Bataan (before we ran out). We received two tablespoons of cereal (cracked wheat, oatmeal, cornmeal, etc.), and a tablespoon of watered-down evaporated milk. Our drink was weak coffee – no milk or sugar. At night it was the same with the addition of a half pear or peach or a spoon of applesauce. The cold storage building was blown up by bombs within a week after I got here, but I'm not sure I ever had anything from it as the soups were so thin and watery it was hard to tell what was in it.

Oh, I almost forgot the bathing facilities. There was only one on the north side of the tunnel. It had a half-inch pipe with a faucet to turn on for a shower of artesian spring water which was salt water mixed with fresh water. The only toilet we had was a 2 or 3 holer with boards on one front end only. No view from the tunnel side. These facilities were for all personnel. This was a busy place except when shells were coming in. With our diet we did not need to go very often. It was hard to keep shaved as there were many trying to get to the one faucet for washing and showers. Flying rocks were coming in too often to go out except for emergencies.

During the last two weeks of April the tunnel became crowded with the various troops who had their artillery guns shot out and no place to hide so they came into the tunnel under the "Rock" where they could get a little rest and a little food. The big doors on each end of the tunnel were almost closed with space for only two persons to go in or out at once. This prevented big and small rocks from coming into the tunnel and thus keep personnel from being killed or wounded as an occasional round or two would hit just above and around the doors. This just cut down the flow of

Chapter 6 Corregidor

clean air, and it was hotter and stickier than ever. There were no air conditioners or fans, except in the General's office – if the electricity was on.

A couple of autos were parked on the "bottom side" road, one about 100 feet away and another one about 200 feet away. Both of the cars looked like giant sieves for fairyland from being hit by flying rock and shrapnel. I think they had been for the Generals, but were not used after the shelling began.

Late one night I helped carry one of the eight men who were caught by shelling, to the hospital tunnel. The weather was clear and HOT. It was hotter inside the tunnel than out in the sun; the air was thick and heavy and impossible to get fresh air or even try for a nap. Circulation was very poor as the winds blew from the wrong direction.

My body, from the top of my head to the soles of my feet, became covered with red spots from heat rash. By this time Japanese shelling had blown away the latrine and the showers, but it was possible to get a canteen of water between incoming shells – if you had the nerve. The water for the island was normally furnished from Mariveles by barge, but there were no more barges. Any trip to the "toilet" behind any big rock was speedy! The machine gun positions outside the doors had been covered with big rocks, but it was not possible to make use of them. My prayers were constant as the shelling never stopped in those last days before the Japanese landed.

No one shaved. The chef must have had water piped into his tiny galley on one side of the tunnel, but the long foot lines took one-half day to be served. Everyone was losing weight and sleep; our haggard appearance was normal.

All bunks were doing double duty as when one got up another was waiting in line would take his place. My spot in the unfinished connecting tunnel was never wanted as it was just too rough. I made out as best I could and got some sleep when the shells and bombs were not coming in. It was always a worry to me that the bombs would make my sleeping spot cave in from the way as the "Rock" would really shake. My prayers were constant as the shelling never stopped in the last days before the Japanese invaded Corregidor.

<u>29 April 1942</u>

This was the Emperor's birthday; in his honor the ferocity of the artillery shells became constant and no one could move outside the tunnel.

<u>30 April 1942</u>

My notes show the bombing and shelling increased from the 15th from one-half sessions to two-hour sessions and then an hour or so of no shelling. In the meantime the bombers would hit the "Rock" but Malinta Tunnel was the prime target; the gun and mortar positions were next. The hospital was being pinched for beds. The floor was also used as the nurses used it to have a place to rest. I wrote Nell a letter, but later knew it would never make it home.

I would often stay up talking to acquaintances. I had seen the Finance Officers and other Colonels destroying Philippine pesos by cutting them up and then a soldier would take the shreds out to be burned. One of the Colonels with a 45-mm pistol would follow to be sure the money was destroyed. Later, in Cabanatuan Prison Camp,

I heard a Navy man claimed he helped find some of the gold that was sunk from the Philippine's Government's Treasury. They were all trained divers (don't remember any of their names), but deliberately lost the bulk of the bullion so the Japanese could not recover it.

2 May 1942

The "Rock," as Corregidor was called, was the target, aided by observation balloons which directed the shelling with damaging accuracy. It was about sundown when I felt an earth-shaking jolt which felt like an earthquake. The men outside near the door came in and reported that the mortar magazine of Battery Geary had been penetrated through 18 feet of concrete and exploded. Men, who had taken shelter in the one with ammunition, were blown to pieces. All the guns except one mortar were knocked out of action. One was blasted off its base, a 20-ton barrel buried in a concrete and steel wall. The survivors from another ammunition magazine, which had been protected with thick concrete and steel doors were badly shaken but made it back into Malinta Tunnel with the information. I don't know how many died, but know the battery was out of action. The shelling by the Japanese increased day and night. They leveled all trees and brush to a maximum of ten inches so it was almost impossible for the men who were manning the guns to make it back into the tunnel. The able-bodied picked up the injured and carried them into the Malinta Tunnel Hospital. The doctors and nurses had a rough time that night

Chapter 7
A Little Bit of History

Gen. MacArthur declared Manila an "Open City" on 26 December 1941. The strategy was to show the Japanese march from Lingayen Gulf so the U.S. and Philippine troops could get to the Bataan Peninsula for a final defense position. Manila radio stations also broadcast the "Open City" messages, but the sad part was the destruction by the Japanese before they entered the city. Much more damage was done when they were forced to retreat when Gen. MacArthur returned as every beautiful, modern city building was blasted by Japanese engineers when they left. Gen. MacArthur's message was sent out from Corregidor as he had moved his staff, family, Philippine politicians, and radio equipment to Malinta Tunnel by 24 December 1941. (This information is from the book "Corregidor, The Saga of a Fortress" by James and William Belote.)

There was a radio bulletin floating around naming KEEL Station in Louisiana as the originator of the headlines: HELP

Chapter 7 A Little Bit of History

IS ON THE WAY. This did nothing to inspire morale as nearly everything was becoming scarce and the enemy was shelling our "last stand" extra heavily. Gen. MacArthur had regularly sent regular radio messages on the air and copies would be distributed on the "Rock." Occasionally they would make it to Bataan where we were fighting the Japanese, but the messages were mere propaganda as there were too many planes shot down; we (the troops on the front line) were holding the Japanese from moving our front lines down to the end of the Peninsula.

Gen. MacArthur, under orders from Franklin D. Roosevelt, left Corregidor on 11 March 1942. "Mac," his wife and son, and staff officers boarded a PT boat which took them to Mindanao, and then the group of 19 people was taken by B-17 bombers to Australia. Upon arrival, MacArthur's message to the troops, Philippines, and the world ended with his well known "I SHALL RETURN!"

Prior to leaving, Gen. MacArthur appointed Gen. Jonathan Wainwright to replace him on Corregidor. Only a very few of the "high brass" knew of this appointment until the "Voice of Freedom" radio station on Corregidor was permitted to air it to the troops fighting on Corregidor and Bataan. I did not know any details until I read it in several different books.

<u>5 May 1942</u>

For the past 5 days there has been continual bombing and 240-mm howitzer shelling from Bataan on the west side and from Cavite on the east side. Today Navy W.O. Robert

Jones and I decided it looked like "tomorrow might not come" so we had the office make up a notice for all Seattle military personnel to meet in the last room of the Malinta Hospital at 8:00 p.m. This was more successful than we dreamed it would be. We called it a meeting for "Seattlelites of Corregidor" and a "get to know your fellow fighters." A sheet was passed around and all names and addresses were taken. Sixteen to 20 people were present. Robert Jones took the list and was to make copies for all. Maj. Paul Wing took pictures, but I never received a copy. It was an hour or more of just getting acquainted. It was mainly officers, but there were several non-commissioned warriors present.

While our meeting was going on the shelling eased up and the Japanese started landing many barge loads of troops on Corregidor. The first landings were on Monkey Point. It is the eastern point of the island. It was not long before firing could be heard by those near the exit doors of the tunnel. It was the Japanese guns from the barges and some machine gun fire from our defenders. This went on until daylight. The Japanese were now less than a mile from the tunnel.

Gen. Wainwright sent Capt. Wade out of the east door with a big white flag of surrender. The first time he was met with many rifle shots landing too close for comfort. He kept the flag and ran back to the tunnel. He waited a half hour or so and went out with the flag again for about 300 yards. He met rifle fire and he speedily returned. As soon as he could talk, I heard him say, "Their aim is getting too good. I threw the flag down." He reported to Gen. Wainwright's office and Gen. Wainwright reported to Gen. MacArthur in Australia. (I have read POW history books which claim other officers took the surrender flag. I was standing on top of a big storage box along the side of the tunnel which made it a good place to see everything that went on and I saw Capt. Wade take out the flag and return without it when the final attempt was made.)

Corregidor fell to the Japanese on 6 May 1942. Remember that this was Philippine time and it was 5 May 1942, in the United States.

GEN. WAINWRIGHT'S MESSAGE TO PRESIDENT ROOSEVELT-

With broken heart and head bowed in sadness but not in shame, I report to your Excellency that today I must arrange terms for the surrender of the fortified island of Manila Bay …

There is a limit of human endurance and that limit has long since been met. Without prospect of relief I feel it is my duty to my country and to the gallant troops to end this useless effusion of blood and human sacrifice …

If you agree, Mr. President, please say to the nation that my troops and I have accomplished all that is humanly possible and that we have upheld our best traditions of the United States and its Army.

May God bless and preserve you and guide you and the nation in the effort to ultimate victory …

With profound regret and with continued pride in my gallant troops I go to meet the Japanese commander …

Goodbye, Mr. President.

PRESIDENT ROOSEVELT'S RESPONSE TO GEN. WAINWRIGHT-

During recent weeks we have been following with growing admiration the day-by-day accounts of your heroic stand against the mounting intensity of bombardment of enemy planes and heavy-siege guns …

In spite of all the handicaps of complete isolation, lack of food and ammunition, you have given the world a shining example of patriotic fortitude and self-sacrifice …

And American people ask no finer example of tenacity, resourcefulness, and steadfast courage. The calm determination of your personal leadership in a desperate situation sets a standard of duty for our soldiers throughout the world …

In every camp and on every naval vessel, soldiers, sailors, and marine are inspired by the gallant struggle of their comrades in the Philippines. The workmen in our shipyards and munitions plants redouble their efforts because of your example …

You and your devoted followers have become a living symbol of our war aims and the guarantee of victory …

Chapter 7 A Little Bit of History

Chapter 8
Prisoner of War

Corregidor was surrendered to the Japanese about noon on 6 May. We were kept in the tunnels and the air was getting very foul and difficult to breathe, especially as the people who smoked were now chain smoking, and there must have been 500 to 600 of us in the Malinta Tunnel alone.

About 2:30 or 3:00 p.m. a couple of Japanese soldiers stuck their heads around the door just enough to peak in. They must have had conversation as they withdrew their heads for a couple of minutes, then came in slowly for about 30 feet. This time they had their flame throwers at ready and they were pointed at the nearest Americans. The crowd in the tunnels immediately gave ground and backed up to give them plenty of space; no one wanted to be "fried" or give any excuse to be killed. One of the Japanese soldiers spoke to a third man and he left the tunnel in a hurry. No action in the tunnel, except for the low buzz of conversation, for

Chapter 8 Prisoner of War

the next half hour. The two soldiers with the flame throwers were constantly on the alert. A Japanese soldier with Captain's bars, his lieutenant, and a message runner, all in combat clothing, then entered. They asked the closest man where the command office was located and were pointed towards Gen. Wainwright's office. The flame throwers opened the way. In about 15 minutes they came back out accompanied by Gen. Wainwright and several of his staff. They went out the north exit with the Captain and his runner. (Later we learned that the Gen. and his staff were taken by auto to Manila for a surrender conference with Gen. Homma.

6 May 1942

This was a "do nothing" day; no cooked food (and very little other food), no water, and no one was able to leave the tunnel, I crawled through "my" connecting tunnel and appropriated two unlabeled cans. A hungry officer friend had a knife for an opener and we enjoyed pears for our dinner. After awhile we ventured into the main tunnel to see what was going on. There were more Japanese in the tunnel, which pushed the crowd back even more so they had more space up to the entrance of the General's offices. I was curious to see what was going to happen, but my hunger and lack of sleep made me decide to crawl back into my "hole in the rock" for some sleep.

7 May 1942 and 8 May 1942

I came out and talked with some of the officers near my hole and received the latest scuttlebutt. The Japanese were clearing the Filipino troops out of the tunnel as it was very crowded. The Japanese were going along the main tunnel and pulling watches off prisoner's arms. Some of the Japanese had watches from their wrists to their armpits and were starting on the other arm. Another prized item was rings the Americans were wearing. It was useless to resist; if a ring was difficult to get off they were ready to cut off the finger. They would gang up on the resisters, force them to the ground, and then use their knives. When they had all the watches and rings in the main tunnel, they searched each tunnel separately for more loot! I did not have a ring or watch so lost nothing.

The American chefs passed out cans of food or someone would find a cache, so I joined in helping to fill my empty stomach. Since there were no more shells coming in we could go outside, find an unused spot, and relieve ourselves. It was a mess but nature had to be satisfied. It was good to get outside into the fresh air and sunshine; it was cooler than the tunnel. Our freedom was soon curtailed as the Japanese began allowing only a few at a time to go out. The entry doors had been partially cleared of boulders so they could be opened by evening. The thick smoke and stale air gradually blew out, but the stinky, ripe smell on us never left as there was no way to bathe.

The Japanese were rounding up the American defenders and taking many of them into the Malinta Tunnel. U.S. Marines as well as G.I.'s (soldiers) came from the east point defense and from many different areas. (It is possible Adolph Richter, Caroline's first husband was one of the Marines but I didn't know any of the men.)

Chapter 8 Prisoner of War

The tunnel was filling again and toilet facilities were non-existent. When it was necessary to go outside you had to find a place inside the circle of Japanese soldiers who guarded the tunnel, and if too many started to come out the guard would stop them until those who had relieved themselves came back in. The bent pipe on the north side still had salty water so you could fill your canteen.

<u>9 May 1942</u>

Very early in the morning the word was passed around to pack up and be ready to move out. "If you cannot carry your possessions, leave them!" So I packed my musette bag with a few toilet items, a couple of shaving razors, my well-worn tooth brush, a small bar of soap I used for washing and also for shaving, three cartons of cigarettes, and a few paper matches, another pair of socks, a small towel, a pencil, a mess kit, spoon, canteen full of water, and a couple cans of food (no labels). In my sack I had a couple of G.I. blankets, a Navy wool blanket, and two sheets. A lot of cotton sheets and blankets, etc., were left behind; I couldn't resist and took some.

I wandered toward the south tunnel entrance as near the exit as I could. In a while the crowd began to move. I was outside in the middle of the group when everyone stopped and a Japanese photographer took our picture. My small Army bag had a couple cans of fruit which I took from the tunnel along with some of my clothes. Upon inspection for guns or knives, a Japanese soldier saw the cans and grunted at me with his hand to take them. I didn't know the "grunts" indicated he wanted me to hand him the tinned fruit. With his rifle butt, he hit my shoulder, knocking me to the ground; kicked me in the ribs, and as he was aiming at my head with the rifle butt again, I moved my head enough so it glanced off my head and hit my neck. I was knocked out. I don't know how many more kicks and rifle butt hits I received – only the fellows that pulled me up knew – but I had big bruises all over my neck, back, arms, hands, ribs, all over my body, stomach, legs, knees, and ankles. Some officers got me up and helped me carry my bags; I was really hurting from the blows and kicks. There were no cans of fruit when I recovered!

Our straggly line of prisoners followed the Japanese non-com until we reached the 92nd Garage, the seaplane base. This was an area of about two city blocks with a big 200x300 foot steel hanger with many loose sheets of corrugated galvanized roofing hanging from the rafters. Some of the sheets were held by only one nail. I went inside the building to get out of the sun. Another reason was that it had a concrete floor. There were no toilet facilities and there was no water. About 12,000 men from every branch of the service were held here for 21 days until the entire Philippine Islands surrendered. There were no Filipinos as they had been separated from us and were being used to clean up Corregidor.

The third day the Japanese allowed 50 men to go with a guard escort to the one slow artesian faucet to fill our canteens or whatever we had to hold water. With thousands needing water and about five escorted "tours" every half hour, there was a continual line for water 24 hours a day.

Chapter 8 Prisoner of War

On the 4th or 5th day, the Japanese finally allowed American Engineers to tap the artesian well with a half-inch pipe into the wire-fenced 92nd Garage area. There never was a time when someone wasn't waiting their turn. It took a long time to fill the 5-gallon cans for the cooks. Our meals were usually rice, or some kind of soup with rice.

10-22 May 1942

The Japanese rounded up the "Rock's" defenders and brought in about 100 into our area. They held back about 200 Americans and hundreds of Filipinos to do cleanup work. We could see them working burying the dead or picking up rifles, or clothing, or on water details the first two days. The area was filthy where the men defecated on the highest part or into the bay. The wave action didn't always take the droppings out of the bay; most of the time it would float back with the next tide. Three big holes were dug on the upper side of the filthy area for toilet use. Within a few days the holes were overflowing and running down the hill, among the prisoners, and in a wide stream across the concrete to the bay.

All the natives were formed into groups of ten for ration serving, thus they tended to establish a small area back-to-back for hanging a couple of blankets on any kind of support they could find for shade. The sun was very hot and it never cooled at night; the concrete was always warm to hot. My first place was in the hanger, but one day the wind blew hard enough to make the big 8' sheet dangerous as it swung in the breeze. I moved outside to the end of the building and made a small patch of grass my hangout. It had a little shade, but was not soiled.

Our biggest problem was the huge flies that multiplied by the millions from the latrines on the hill. We always said that the flies had superiority! They would land on our faces and hands – any skin exposed – and try to bite. When we had food they were the bravest flies we ever encountered and we waved our hands across our food containers continually to keep them off the food. Sometimes they would land on my spoon before I could get it into my mouth – it was no joke when you clomped your teeth on a fly. It happened to me several times. Mosquitoes were also eating us, especially at night when we tried to sleep.

In the evening, the second day in my new holding area, I decided to wash my sweaty body. This was before we had any running water so I went to the bay and stepped into the edge up to my knees, dipped my small towel into the water and washed my face and chest before I saw the feces in the water. I just wrung out my towel and dried off. About 4 days later I began to get infections on my face and chest. By then we had clean water and I tried to wash my face and chest, but it did no good; each day became worse. I looked horrible but didn't know what to do. We had no doctors. After the first week my feet and legs began to swell and my dysentery began acting up. Six to eight trips per day to the "john" were normal.

<u>23 May 1942</u>

After our meager breakfast of lugau (lugau is a watery rice gruel) we received instructions to "pack up, we are going to

Chapter 8 Prisoner of War

move." Where? That's a silly question as the Japanese do not give information! Our "Nip" guides with their rifles and bayonets at the ready took us to the south dock on Corregidor. There were two boats at the dock, each about 100 feet long. We were told to sit down just off the dock. I sat down just a few feet from the entry to the dock. The sun was hot – just as hot as the days before. We just sat, talked, and speculated what the Japanese were planning. Lunch time went by without food or water. Fortunately I had filled my canteen and I was very careful not to drink it all at once. Our evening cup of lugau never arrived. We sat and waited. Toilet facilities were the usual; do it where ever you can. Sitting in the sun made my infection spread all the way down the front of my body; I must have smelled as bad as the latrines we left behind. We wait until ALL the 92nd Garage POWs had arrived and then they started loading the two boats. I was not the first to load in spite of my close position. The holds were filled and the last aboard had to find a place on the deck. I was lucky to find a spot about 20 feet from the bow. My dysentery was bad, but I could just "stick my uncovered butt" over the side. This was S.O.P. (Standard Operating Procedure) with the Japanese. I was lucky as below decks there were no buckets for toilet use, just the floor! Late that evening the props began to turn and we were on our way. No Filipino troops were aboard these two ships.

24 May 1942

About 9:00 a.m. the boat dropped anchor. We were told to get off. The happy Japanese guards helped us get off the boat – if you didn't jump promptly, they would give you a big shove and you landed in the salt water of Manila Bay. Then it was either walk or swim the 20 to 50 feet until you reached dry land. The salt water soaked not only you but everything you were carrying. Walking in shoes filled with salt water was awful.

The Japanese took the long way (six miles) to Bilibid Prison to show off the defeat of the "mighty Americans," and they made the Filipinos line the streets all the way to the abandoned prison. Many of the Filipinos would secretly show the "V" for Victory sign and many were crying. If we slowed down or talked to any Filipinos we were struck with rifle butts. The POWs who fell down due to sickness, starvation, and lack of strength were picked up in a truck and unloaded at the gate of the prison. A new prison construction was begun in 1936. The remnants of the old prison were used as a detention center then known as the Manila City Jail.

26 May 1942

The floor in Bilibid Prison was concrete and after three days I began to get sore spots on my ankles, thigh bone, elbows, and shoulders. It was common in all of Bilibid and I found out most prisoners were using their clothes rolled up to pad the pressure points. It was difficult to get sound sleep when you were not active, but that changed when I got into work details. This is the main prison in the Philippines. Hard-core prisoners: murderers, rapists were sent down to a different prison. We just sat around and slept on concrete floors.

We were not allowed to go on details so this was a really

Chapter 8 Prisoner of War

boring time for us. I know I just lived from day to day.

28 May 1942

One work crew of prisoners came in before it was dark and I met Lt. Al Herbold again. Al and his sergeant were the men who started to swim to Corregidor when my sergeant and I did. This is his story: They swam about a mile and turned left when they saw a PT boat anchored along the shore hidden from the planes under overhanging trees. They went aboard and stayed hidden until the next night when they started toward Mindanao and points south. They hoped to get to Australia. Everything was going well; they made it through mines past Corregidor and were in open channel for the next island, trying to slip by the Japanese destroyers patrolling the channel. A shot went across the bow of their PT boat. They changed directions but the destroyer was faster with more powerful guns than the PT boat so they surrendered and were taken aboard the destroyer. They ended up in Bilibid Prison and were made to work on anything the Japanese wanted done. I know that Lt. Herbold did not make it back to the United States.

Lt. Herbold talked the Japanese guard into allowing me to go into the workmen's area which was in the inner part of the prison cells. I grabbed my bag and went with him to his area. Here they had a shower and a better ration of food (more lugau and soup with vegetables) than the outer compound. By getting a shower a day, soap, and a goodnight's sleep, my infected scabs had almost disappeared and I felt more like a living person. After work in the evening, I played chess with a Navy commander, washed my few clothes, or just "loafed."

While at Bilibid with work details we were taken by truckload of 15-20 POWs to the Port of Manila to handle cargo into and out of Manila, which included 100-kilo bags of rice, heavy tobacco bundles, other food stuffs and scrap iron. Army and Navy canned foods and other supplies were taken by the Japanese for their own use. One day, while loading cartons of evaporated milk out of Rizal Stadium rooms under the bleachers, I stole a can of milk and opened it with a nail. I was caught drinking it in the toilet room. The Japanese gave me many "kendo stick" strikes across my head, neck, back, arms and legs; also was hit with the rifle butt across my back. I hit the floor but slowly got up to work and made it to the end of the day. I was glad to get away from this group of guards when the truck was loaded for Bilibid Prison at the end of the day.

The Japanese soldiers would harass the enlisted men to Sumo Wrestle with them. They would pick a medium-size man so they could throw them to the ground. Big Americans were also challenged but, if they were smart, they would let the Japanese throw them; if an American won. The biggest Japanese would be found to take on the American winner.

I had been in work parties all over Manila, but about 15 June I came down with fever, chills; severe pains in my body, and all my bones ached. A Navy doctor made a tentative diagnosis of Dengue Fever (result of mosquito born disease and/or virus, and possibly complicated by malaria. With the aid of Quinine, I began to improve in a few days, but was not sent back to work. Anyway fewer men were being sent

Chapter 8 Prisoner of War

to work as they were beginning to cut the work force.

25 June 1942

The sickest men were cut first, next those that were the slowest and weakest; all were transferred back to the "big outside compound." This was where the transferred prisoners were kept and then shipped out to various work details away from Manila or to other POW camps. While I was waiting in the big compound a large group of American troops were brought in. Many were from the large #1 hospital in Bataan. I met Capt. Edwin Burk from Brainerd, Minnesota again of the 194th Tk. Co. A. Many were in very poor health.

26 June 1942

This morning we were awakened early and names of prisoners to be moved out were called. My name was called and I moved my few belongings to a different area in the compound. When 200 men's names had been called the guards formed us into a row and we marched to "Tootabon" railroad station. There the Japanese soldiers forced about 75 men into the small steel box cars. The last men were forced inside with rifle blows to the "standing room only" car. I was lucky and had only ONE rifle butt blow on my back. They then locked the steel doors. There was no water, no toilet facilities, and very little air. The outside temperature was 98º F and being in packed steel cars was like being in an oven. Men had to relieve themselves where they stood, or literally climb over the others to get a little crack under the door where the urine would run out. Those with dysentery had to relieve themselves where they stood. We stayed at "Tootabon" for maybe four hours and then began to move. We later found out it was a 90-100 km ride to Tarlac. By then we were wet with perspiration and weak from lack of water and food.

Seven hours after we loaded, the doors opened and the guards helped us unload using kicks for those who didn't move fast enough. We later heard they had a truck for those who couldn't walk or passed out on the 5-mile hike to Cabanatuan, our new prison camp.

Chapter 8 Prisoner of War

Chapter 9
Cabanatuan
Prisoner of War Camp

Cabanatuan had been a Philippine Army mobilization and training base and was 600 by 800 yards in area. The compound was surrounded by a barbed wire fence and guarded by Japanese sentries in 20-foot high towers and machine gun pits. Americans were segregated from their Filipino comrades. This camp is located about 40 miles from Fort Stotsenberg and north of Manila. John M. Stotsenberg was a Capt. of the Philippine Department's 26th Calvary, 86th Field Artillery Regiment and the 88th Field Artillery Regiment. He was a Col. of the First Nebraska Volunteers. He was killed on 23 April 1899, at age 40.

My guess is there were about 30 main barracks, 15 on each side of the road which would hold up to 10,000 or more, plus many extra smaller barracks which housed the guards and the Japanese camp officers. The buildings were made of split bamboo strips spaced approximately ¼-inch apart on a framework of floor joists for the main floor. The outside walls were of Swali (split woven bamboo) about 6 feet high, 3/8-inch thick, and ten feet wide. Along the sides they had made a shelf of split bamboo about 16 inches off the floor and 8 feet deep. Another shelf of the same depth was anchored to the main posts holding up the roof that had ladders every 20 feet or so which the prisoners used to get to their upper bunks. The roof was made from heavy bundles of Cogan grass or rice straw.

There was only one kitchen for the prisoner's food preparation which consisted of lugau (soft over-cooked rice, very few vegetables (daikons – long white Japanese radishes) and sweet potato greens or other greens were the vegetables) in lots of water and called soup!

Before we were assigned to one of the barracks we were taken to a vacant area just before the main compound gate. The guards made us line up and spread all our possessions for them to inspect. There must have been more than 20 rows which stretched for 100 feet or so. The "inspectors" came by and "appropriated" knives, scissors, cameras, guns, cigarettes, and any other item which took their fancy. Watches and rings (for the few who still had them) disappeared fast.

We received two meals a day of steamed rice, occasionally accompanied by fruit, soup, or meat. To supplement our diet, we were able to smuggle food and supplies hidden in our underwear into the camp during Japanese-approved trips into town. We collected food using a variety of methods including stealing, bribing guards, planting gardens, and killing animals that entered the camp such as mice, snakes, ducks, and stray dogs.

Multiple escapes were made throughout the history of the prison camp, but the majority ended in failure. In one attempt, four soldiers were recaptured by the Japanese. The guards forced all prisoners watch as the four soldiers were beaten, forced to dig their own graves, and then executed.

Then a welcome to "misery land" by the commanding officer of Cabanatuan Prison Camp was done. It began with the words "You are HOSTAGES; you are not prisoners of war. Remember, you are hostages and you must obey all our orders!" We believed very strongly that he was speaking for the Japanese Army AND the Japanese Government. He continued: "You will be assigned in groups of ten. If any one of you escapes – or tries to escape – the others will be shot. If you miss "Tinko" (morning and evening lineup for counting off) you will be punished. Also, you must salute ALL Japanese you meet. This means you must bow to all officers and also salute. If you do not obey ALL orders you will be punished."

By this time those that were weakest had fallen to the ground but the Japanese commander didn't stop talking and he was getting hoarse and losing volume on the last half of the welcome was lost. We didn't "give a damn" anyway; all we wanted was a place to lie down as we were tired, hungry, thirsty, and dirty. We were finally given a Baihai (barracks) number and our "group of 10 numbers" and off we went to the barracks. Since we were late, only a few had weak lugau soup.

Chapter 9 Cabanatuan Prisoner of War Camp

Most of us were interested in getting water to drink. I took the water route and went to sleep.

Many of the American POWs were in a critical state of physical exhaustion and mental depression when they arrived at the Cabanatuan Prison Camp. Most had been in continuing combat for months, fighting on empty stomachs, against overwhelming odds. The men knew that they had been cut off from any reinforcements of men or supplies after Pearl Harbor. They fought with what they had to slow down the Japanese invasion and give our nation more time to mobilize. The price our men paid for their efforts was evident as they shuffled into the Cabanatuan Prison Camp looking like walking skeletons. The makeshift prison hospital was filled with as many as 2500 patients. The daily death rate in the camp ran as high as 60. The death toll during the June to December 1942 period from untreated wounds, tropical diseases, malnutrition, and starvation, neglect, and Japanese brutality was estimated to be 2300! The Japanese issued documents certifying that each death was caused by malaria beriberi, pellagra, diphtheria; in fact, anything but the real cause – starvation and malnutrition, Death hit the youngest men the hardest. Of the men who died during July 1942 at the #1 Camp, 85% were under 30. The dead were buried in mass graves within the camp.

27 June 1942

Our first meeting "Tinko" head count was early. I know I had to hurry just to make it off the upper sleeping shelf for the count off. One of my shelf mates was John L. Kierman, a stenographer for the Benquet Gold Mine in Baguio, Philippines. My number in the barracks was 72, but we just listened to the number of the man next to you and then said our number. We had to memorize the count in Japanese up to 100. One to 10 was as follows: iehi, ni, san, shi, go, roku, sichi, hachi, ku, ju. Seventy-two was sichi ju ni. The Japanese guard checked his roster each time we counted off, morning and night.

There was a water faucet near our baihai with a small stream flowing. There was only one more faucet at the lower end of the camp. These two faucets would serve up to 7,000 POWs. Many times during the day the faucet would be turned off so the Japanese would have water for their kitchen as well as our cooks for the camp who needed water for their many caldrons. I finally learned to brush my teeth, shave, take a "wash-down" bath and have a couple of mouths-full to drink from my one pint Army cup. In very hot weather, sun all day with high humidity, it was easy to perspire a couple pints in the afternoon. I got in line frequently to get more water.

Each barracks had a man to get the bucket of rice and one man for a bucket of soup (well, it was called soup – by some!) One person dished out the rice and the next man dipped and poured the soup, if you didn't have a container you were skipped. Some only had a used tin can they picked up some place.

Today was also a day of rumors; the latest "pipe dream" was that the Japanese were going to exchange us for prisoners the U. S. had taken.

I had been in Cabanatuan for a few days when I was

put on a work detail. I don't remember the first few days, but do remember the first time I helped carry one of the unfortunate "O" ward patients to be buried. We had an old wood door and his body was put in the middle with his old blanket covering him. It was the usual hot steamy day; my costume was only a "G" string, and the trail was well worn for about a half mile. The weight really got to my arms and back before we came to the grave, which was a huge pit dug in the soil and through some clay that made a big mound on the sides. The flies were terrific, even though the many bodies were partly covered with soil. We dumped our load and got out as fast as we could; the blanket was saved to be washed and used again in the hospital.

27 June to about 27 July 1942

Some of the fellows I enjoyed chatting with when not on work detail were men from the Benquet Gold Mind. John L. Kiernan, and engineers W. L, Northby, George D. Couch, and James D. Lynch, also 2nd Lt. Benjamin F. VanSant, who was deserted at night by his Filipino troops while searching for defense positions along the river when he suddenly met the Japanese coming over the river bank. He pulled his 45 cal. pistol and shot until his shells were gone. Turning to run he was caught by the Japanese who had circled behind him. They wanted him for interrogation; he didn't know enough, but was kept a prisoner as it was early in the Bataan invasion. Louis T. Lazzarini, Chemical War Service Captain, always said the Pacific War would last 3 to 5 years. This estimate was made before any news was known of the European situation.

We would get together to discuss topics such as rumors of health, sick bay in hospital, the men in the upper shelves who were sick with dysentery, malaria, etc., and the effect on the men below; the death rates in camp, burial sites, war situation, our lack of support from the USA, and RELIGION. Hospital wards "O" through "OOO" were having only about 15 deaths a day

All "hostages" were in a 10-man security group, recorded by name. If any man in this group escaped, the other 9 would be executed (if the escapee was not caught). It had happened once before I arrived and they were still holding the nine men as the hostages had not yet been found. Our weather had been pouring rain with hot sun in between, but today (19 July) is "hot as Hades." The sun had heated the body as it was decaying causing it to float to the top. The belief was that the man had gone to the toilet at night while it was raining and then slipped into the latrine on slick clap mound around it. Nine men were very relieved this afternoon when the missing man was found floating in one of the 10x10-foot latrines! The men were released from detention, returned to their barracks, and another man was assigned to make up the 10-man group.

An escape attempt was made on 20 August by Lt. Col. Biggs, Lt. Gilbert, USN, and Lt. Col. Breitung. All hostages were informed by the Japanese commanders upon arrival in prison camp and repeated and each time we moved to another location. The three men were caught and stripped to shorts and tied to posts by the gate. They were beaten from head to foot and the bloody men were left in the sun without food or water for two days. No one was allowed to help them in any way. Each change of guard would beat them unmercifully and the hot sun left them blistered. We heard that Col. Biggs was taken out of camp and beheaded; the other two were taken around the hill from camp and shot. No POWs were witnesses but they never showed up in camp again. This was the Japanese's way of teaching us not to attempt to escape.

Talented men headed by Col. "Zerb" Wilson presented many good shows with men who had been able to bring in a few musical instruments. I remember mouth organs and a ukulele. The shows were held at the north end of the officer's barracks on a sloping hill and they were so good for our morale.

18 July 1942

This was my last day on burial detail. I pooped out and dropped my end of the load. It had rained and the trail was very slippery and I fell in the mud. I received 4 or 5 "kendo" stick hits across my back and neck to help me to keep up with the burial line. I had been turning yellow and didn't know what the problem was. I found Dr. Hickman from our 194th tank unit and he said I had hepatitis which can affect the liver. My appetite was getting worse each day; I was forcing myself to eat my lugau but it was getting hard each day to finish it. The hepatitis kept getting worse and I had a rough time going along the slippery trail to the canteen and almost fell in. Nausea makes it difficult to eat even a little of the lugau and Dr. Hickman suggested that I thoroughly wash some charcoal clean and chew it well with the lugau to get it down. It was one of the hardest things I have ever done, but I did it and in a few days began to improve. By 25 July I was back to eating and trying to make up some weight loss.

I mentioned wearing a "G" string. Because I was not able to carry many clothes when I was fighting in Bataan and when I swam to Corregidor, and when I was taken prisoner, my clothes were becoming quite tattered. I, as well as many others, wore "G-strings" made of strips of very thin cotton cloth about 12 inches wide and 30 inches long, tied about the waist and pulled up between the legs. The "G-string" was a small cover and did not help with sunburn or keep the pesky flies and insects away!

1 August 1942

When it rained, it poured and it was not warm so we really didn't like rain except to get a shower bath under the eaves of our Baihai. Maybe five times I stood under the eaves and scrubbed as hard and as fast as I could as I was shivering. This was also a good time to wash dirty pants because of accidents with dysentery, or if I fell into the latrine overflow which ran through camp. Navigating on a dark night without a moon was hazardous. The clay heaped along the side for a trail from the ditch was as slippery as wet soap.

Another health problem was swelling in my legs. Work details outside the camp could secretly make contact with the Filipinos for food, sugar, cigarettes, or cigars, etc. The men in the work party would help me and I was able to get a bottle of Quinine and a box of cigars. Sugar was brought in by many workers which they made into candy and which, at first, sold for $1.00, then $2.50 each piece (U.S. money). This lasted about a week, then no more sugar. I was using the dried, uncured tobacco for my pipe as smoking a little made it easier to keep living on short rations.

2-19 August 1942

During this period many rumors flew around the camp such as "all colonels would be shipped to Japan." With the troops scheduled to leave camp the Japanese decided to cut the rice ration and were cut in half until the men actually shipped out. There was no change in our lugau diet, but the soup was now very often without vegetables, and then came the days when only hot water was served as soup. To help myself I picked up the peelings of potatoes that were thrown into the garbage pit inside the fence from the Japanese's kitchen window. I needed several hours to peel the peelings and get a canteen full of edible peelings. I then cooked them over a small fire back of the baihais so the smoke would not alert the guards. The saltless potatoes tasted good and cut my hunger pangs a little. Sometimes I found a scrap of vegetable that I could wash with the potato peelings and have a tastier saltless feast!

The Quinine I had received I shared with two friends: Lt. Gaskil and Lt. John Kirmen. When that was gone I was again at the mercy of the malaria-carrying mosquitoes. During this time I had my first bout with malaria with fever and chills for the next 3 to 4 days. Also, my teeth wee getting loose; I could wiggle them with my tongue. Dr. Hickman said it was caused by lack of Vitamin Cl. (slows down or causes cell damage).

20 August to 2 September 1942

I finally moved from my Baihai to a small one nearby. There were only four of us in this small house. The daily routine went on. The rumor for technical men was now a reality. They were identified and took the "glass rod" test performed by the Japanese doctors. My malaria flare-ups came every month. Burial details were still going on, but the lines were a little shorter. The hospital across the road still had a large number of patients. Some late comers brought the word that a Tayabaz, Philippine Island, work detail of 300 had had 93 deaths and many very sick were left in Bilibid when this group came to Cabanatuan.

3 September to 6 October 1942

We heard the last group of technical men left camp for Japan. Now there is a list of 500 officers to go to Mindanao and 500 officers for destinations in Japan. My name was on for Mindanao. Lt. Nichol wanted to go to Mindanao so I traded with him. It was easy, just ask! It was one of the best moves I ever made.

There have been more guerrillas in the vicinity and rumors are the Japanese don't like it. Food servings are less and less.

21 October 1942

The wood detail came in this evening at 5:00 p.m. as usual with their trailer load of wood for the kitchen cooks.

Rumor was the guards caught one of the Filipino guerrillas and cut off his head. One of the guards carried it on top of a long pole for all to see, and then stood it by the office of the camp commander. It was close to the gate into our fenced area.

One of the lieutenants was sick and had just received his lugau but had not eaten it. He lay down and was dead by the time we had finished eating. We called the commander for our 10-man security group to report it, and the body was taken to the hospital group for the next burial. We divided his food and blankets. I got his mosquito net and could again sleep without feeding the local bugs and mosquitoes. However, the malaria chills and fever hit me again.

1 November 1942

I was transferred from Group 2 to Group 1. Rumor had it that Group 1
(about 1300 men) was being sent to Japan. Cigarettes (Filipino) were being traded for clothing, which didn't bother me as I didn't have any (my diary says). First the Japanese doctor gave me a shot in the arm. Then I had to drop my pants to the ground, bend over, and a Japanese corpsman shoved a glass rod up my rectum. He rubbed the feces on a glass test plate and placed my name and number on it. The next day we had the glass rod test again. In spite of the poor state of health no one flunked the test! We were all considered able to work.

The following day we marched across the road to the area where we hear our "welcome" speech. We spread out our worldly goods for another search and were ordered to take off all our clothes and place them in front of our blankets. The Japanese picked up our clothing and gave us a new pair of pants and shirts made of blue denim. All the clothing were Filipino troop training outfits and were all at least two sizes too small. It made no difference to the Japanese and they made us go back to our baihai. I ditched most of the blue denim issued to me and put on my last pair of pants which I had smuggled through the inspection.

5 November 1942

After morning lugau with 500+ POWs with our meager sacks of possessions, assembled, and again given a speech by the Japanese colonel in which he reiterated that we were HOSTAGES AND NOT PRISONERS OF WAR. They would never call us POWs; it was always hostages. We were marched to Tarlac where we were shoved into steel box cars for a steamy ride to Manila. We had no water or food on the trip. We arrived late that day and walked to Pier seven. The night was spent on the pier with guards keeping us in one big group. Our meal that night was a big deep pan of steamed fish covered with flies. Almost all of us got dysentery. About dusk we watched the guards walk around a stack of bales and boxes, completing the circle about every 5 to 10 minutes. We were curious so I took an old razor blade and cut a hole in the bag so it couldn't be seen by the guards, reached in and pulled out a couple bunches of dry cured tobacco. I concealed the tobacco under my coat until I could hide it in my bag. Another prisoner watched me and

did the same thing. I made one more trip and brought back three bunches, which made a big load. By the next morning the dysentery was in full force and we were lined up using the one toilet on the pier. The long lines were terrible and there was no paper!
NAGATA MARU

6 November 1942

After our "lunch" of lugau we were lined up to board the ship the NAGATA MARU. My notes say, "maybe 6 or 7 tons" for the ship. Little did I know the ship was at least 200 or maybe 250 feet long. It was an old freighter with rusty steam pipes wrapped with burlap and "something" to help stop the steam from leaking and burning the sailors. The steam hoist was broken and it was well after dark before we sailed. We were taken to the forward hold which was two decks deep with two side wall shelves on each side about 8 feet off the deck. We had a 20-foot steel ladder to reach the bottom which still had the manure from the horses it had transported. NO sanitary facilities. A couple of buckets were sent down for the first 60 POWs to arrive. It was real difficult and a hazard to the men below when we tried to empty the full buckets!

The Japanese soldiers forced everyone into the hold by filling the side wall shelf first, and then the deck. It all began by having us stand very close together in a solid mass, and then two Japanese soldiers entered the hold and used their rifles to convince the standing to get closer together. Two more Japanese were on deck and used their rifle butts on heads and hands to get the POWs down into the hold; the last man going down was hit really hard, forcing him to let go and fall on the others, causing all to fall in a domino effect. The pileup injured many. I noticed what was being done and stalled as long as possible and then went down; I received only one hit on the side of my head and shoulders. When all 600 were in the hold, deck planks were installed except for two that were left with one end open for air and a way to pass food and water to the men in the hold. Two machine gunners on the captain's deck guarded the holds.

At first we could only sit between the legs of the man behind us and sleep sitting up. Needless to say everyone was not able to use the buckets to urinate or for the dysentery that was rampant. The smell became something you would never want to endure again. Our chow was large pails of miso soup and a bucket of rice the first day.

Over the big hold of the ship there was a crossways steel beam that supported 3-inch thick by 12 inches wide by 20 feet long wood planks from the forward edge of the hold to the middle, and another from the middle to the aft edge. At certain times, such as air or submarine attacks, these planks were then covered with a heavy tarp. The Japanese allowed two planks to be open over our ladder for air and to be able to come to the top when we needed to go to the two "potties," wood outhouses with a roof, hanging over the side. It was a "thrill" when you sat down over the hole and the ship would roll, or due to a tilt from a slack support line, you would feel like you were going overboard.

I heard that the next 700 POWs arrived late that afternoon

and were shoved into the aft hold. It wasn't until later that I found out they were enlisted men. On a fun trip to the Philippines in 1977 I met Fred and Virginia Pemberton.

7 November 1942

We got underway about noon. There were 15 ships and one destroyer in our group. A few POWs were lucky to be allowed on deck as we sailed past Corregidor and out into the South China Sea – I wasn't one of them!

This first night we tried to sleep sitting up but often fell over on the next man's leg. We tried to sleep in snatches. Somewhere the next morning (8 November) off the Philippine Islands after our morning rice we were allowed in small groups to come up on the deck for some air and to wash out our dirty shorts and pants in salty sea water. I hung my shorts on the rail and they floated off on a brisk puff of wind. While I waited for my pants to dry I wrapped myself in beautiful wool Navy blanket that had been abandoned by someone while leaving Corregidor and I had picked it up. A load of disabled Japanese soldiers were on their way home on the Nagata Maru and one of them came by, grabbed my blanket, jerked it hard enough so I fell on the deck with only my shirt for cover. The Japanese promptly went down into his hold with my blanket. Was he really a DISABLED soldier?

I'll never know. All I could do was rescue my wet pants, go back to the hold to my stuff and get another blanket. I learned from another prisoner that it was best to put some sticky oatmeal cereal on your blanket in spots and stain it yellow; no one will steal your blanket or clothing. A smart artillery officer had done it on Corregidor before surrender when we still had a little oatmeal in our diet. It was no help to me now.

After a few days we discovered we had unwelcome guests – body lice were prevalent and could feed without us feeling them. We carried them until we arrived in Zentauji POW camp many months later. We had one light bulb in the middle of the hold – maybe a 60 watt – but with all the dirt it was just a glimmer of light.

8 November 1942

I was ready to take my turn on deck when the submarine alarm went off.

Activity sounds on deck were many with thumping of feet and shouts of "hostages" coming up the ladder almost on top of each other, with the guards rushing them with their rifles. The planks were dropped into place and the canvas tarp wedged down tight. There was a hot sun on deck and body heat in the hold was soon suffocating. The air was so foul and the lack of oxygen made some frantic and they screamed for air. It was difficult to get the Japanese to open the hatch, even after their "Y" guns had quit shooting charges at the submarine. Finally, the hatch was opened one plank width only. It wasn't enough. It was not until there were two dead in the hold before they allowed the second plank to be opened. Dead were two lieutenants: Lt. Danka and another I did not know. An American colonel finally convinced the Japanese captain to allow a wind sock to be installed so air could be funneled into the hold. (See more information about 8 November under 7 November 1942.)

9 November 1942

The NAGATA MARU pulled into the tiny harbor of Taikao (now renamed Kachsiung by the Chinese), and Taiwan, the most southern port, where all Japanese ships stopped for supplies on their way from the South China Sea. Most of the ship's officers and part of the higher-ranking crew went ashore. That afternoon a truck with some kind of supplies was loaded on board. Next truck loads of coal were unloaded into another hold. The POWs were chased away from the loading hoist crane and the steam lines which had extremely hot spray squirting out in many places from the rusty pipes. I was amazed the ship could still float – it was long overdue for the Davy Jones Locker!

The weather was beautiful, sunny, and the salty air smell mingled with the smell from the garbage and sewage floating in the water. The day was enjoyable as we could be on deck most of the time. After the noon chow of rice and miso soup we finished cleaning up the best we could in salt water. Most of the time was spent talking with other "hostages" in our group as we could not go into any other part of the ship. Our area was forward of the captain's bridge with 27-mm machine guns on each side pointed at our hold. They were able to cover the entire forward deck area and manned 24 hours a day. In addition, there were guards with rifles and bayonets to work on us at the slightest provocation. As the sun sank low, the guards chased anyone on deck below, where we struggled to get some sleep only after finding our sack of belongings had been moved from our usual spot.

10 November 1942

This was another hot day. Most of us got on deck once more. I sunburned as I stripped to my "G-string" to wash my pants again. The soil included some of the horsy stuff in the hold, usual dysentery problems, as well trying to kill body lice eggs and any live lice running around on me with a load of my blood – I'm a mess!

Late in the afternoon the ship's officers and crew returned. Most were drunk and in a sour mood. Immediately all POWs were ordered into the hold and orders must have included beating us as we scampered down the ladder into the hold. Scuttlebutt was that the Japanese had suffered some losses in the South Pacific. (Much later we found out they had indeed lost many ships and lives in a battle somewhere in the South Pacific.) The hatch was battened down, the heat built up, and the still air didn't flow into the wind sock until the sun went down and one plank was opened for air. That was the least they could do as we didn't have any water or food that night.

My malaria came on again and I alternately froze (it felt like it) and then burned up with fever. I didn't get much sleep that night.

11 November 1942

Another day without food or water; most canteens were empty; more die.

The Japanese refused to allow us to dump the pails of

toilet waste and the waste overflowed onto the dock where we walked and some had to sleep. What a mess! Late in the day the water and a chance to empty overflowing pails were allowed. A plea to remove the dead was refused —- we could not dump them into the harbor.

12 November 1942

No morning chow and two more "hostages" died. Water was finally allowed.

Weather was hot and the smell must have been blowing up to the crew. We sailed in the afternoon. When the boat cleared the harbor it began to roll. Our noon food came and the "honey buckets" (toilet waste) were dumped overboard and returned. The dead were allowed to be brought out of the hold. This activity was done by physically stronger officer volunteers; none of the work was done by the Japanese crew. Sometime in the afternoon the dead were buried at sea. My notes do not indicate the dates the men died, but do show that a total of eight were buried at sea. Many were sick, including me.

13-15 November 1942

There is a usual routine now. We are allowed on deck. It is raining and
 blowing very hard; it is almost impossible to use the deck toilets. The spray hits the boards on the side of the toilets and the salt water comes in; the deck is slick and very difficult to hang on to pails for food or dump the "honey buckets." The farther we go, the rougher it becomes.

I ventured on deck and could see the big waves breaking over several small islands about two miles away. They had enough strength after going over the islands to hit the side of the ship and still splash onto the deck. I suspected it was a typhoon. Knowledgeable naval officers confirmed my suspicions; they also said we were lucky to have made it between the islands and the main island of Taiwan so the waves were somewhat broken. We sat in the lee of the islands with eight other Japanese ships heading to Taipei, Taiwan or to Moji, Japan. We were cooped up with a minimum opening into the hold and for five days were given a good rocking and patching. Any deck activity such as carrying chow pails or emptying "honey buckets" soaked you immediately by the hard blowing wind and heavy rain.

The convoy took off as soon as they were able and headed off for the next destination. More POWs ("hostages") died and were committed to the sea. Late one afternoon the siren blew and the "Y" guns shot their depth charges. We were locked in the hold and could only pray we would not be sunk.

In the midst of the activity we heard a loud noise somewhere near the middle of the ship and we could only hope the torpedo did not detonate. This was another terrifying close call for me and there was nothing I could do about it. It was up to God. The Japanese were stomping around the deck above us plenty fast, so we knew they were as scared as we were. Fortunately for us, this was the last submarine attack we encountered.

Chapter 9 Cabanatuan Prisoner of War Camp

26 November 1942

We arrived at Moji, Japan late in the afternoon and the ship docked next to a huge warehouse. It was unloaded and we took our worldly goods and exited our "Hell Ship." The weaker were helped by the stronger men as the cold air poured into the hold and we hurried to get out. It was so cold we shivered and stumbled as we stepped on the gang plank. Some slipped and barely escaped falling into the water. The guards indicated an area along the side of the warehouse for us to sit down. We waited a couple of hours sitting on our bags and trying to keep warm in our tropical clothing. The cold wind was brutal. While we were sitting the guards again searched us. Thankfully, no contraband was found. We pulled our blankets out of our bags and wrapped up in them for a little warmth. The ice was thick on the dock and very difficult to walk on. Many fell and had to be helped up.

Chapter 10
TANAGAWA POW CAMP

27 November 1942

This morning the guards woke us early. We did not respond in the usual fast Army fashion. Many were sick; all were tired, and weak from lack of food. The guards soon had us all up and began lining us up into groups. At last the "forward march" was given by the Japanese officer and we were led to the ferry dock. The dock was one or two miles away but it seemed like 10! As the last of the 1,300 or more POWs arrived, so did the ferry. (One source "The Japanese Story" by Med-Search, printed in 1980, reported over 100 or more sick men were left on the dock; they were taken away but were never seen again.)

Loading began shortly after a small group of Japanese unloaded. A few looked like business men but the balance was laborers or farmers. The first on took the upper deck bench seats and the last took the deck below, some sat on benches and the balance on the floor. The ferry headed for Shimoneseki on the Island of Honshu.

From the dock it was a short walk to the train station. We sat around in one of the big rooms until the train arrived. The passenger cars were very nice; it was their first-class 100-mile speed train, but it didn't go that fast with us. It stopped too many places for passengers or other items such as mail. When the train pulled out of the station we were given a "Binto Box" for breakfast and every grain of rice was eaten. We spent the night on the train with another Binto Box for evening chow. We couldn't read the name of the towns on the stops, but Kobe and Osaka were in big American letters.

28 November 1942

We unloaded, went through the station, and waited on the street car side.

The street cars were like the Toonerville Trolley; one big set of four wheels and a long body that hung over the set of wheels. I don't know how many trolleys it took to get us to the end of the track to the south of Osaka along the sea coast. Each trolley unloaded, and then was moved to a switch on another track for its return trip.

The camp guards escorted us about a mile towards the sea to a new camp called Tanagawa. There were barracks all new and clean, some with dirt floors, none with heat; some smaller buildings, including the cook house, the camp commander's hangout, a big outhouse with 20+ seats, and a hospital section. I use the word hospital very loosely. The Japanese use only one style of building: rectangular with open center aisle full length. The barracks contained a continuous bunk on each side about 10 inches off the floor, with a second set of sleeping bunks accessible by ladders about eight feet from the dirt floor. There was NO heat summer or winter! As I remember they had stucco walls and a thatched roof. It was cold when we arrived but a hot cup of tea helped thaw us out with our serving of rice for our evening meal.

29 November 1942

Ten of the very ill were sent to the hospital in Osaka. None returned and the camp commander said all had died. As soon as our rice and miso-flavored hot water was eaten we were "allowed" to strip outside in the wind and 20-something degree weather and take a bath from a small bucket of hot water. This was supposed to help us get rid of the body and head lice we had picked up in the hold of the Nagata Maru. It didn't work. The bath didn't take long; most of the men didn't have towels anyway, and we just hurried to put our lice-infested clothing back on. The so-called baths took the whole day as we had to heat more water for all to bathe. The very sick were sent to the hospital without baths.

The buildings were flimsily constructed with dirt floors and paper-thin walls coming about 6 inches off the floor. The barracks were very cold and had no heat so it was very, very cold with temperatures falling below freezing so the conditions were pretty tough. There were 2 decks of bunks with a ladder going up every 20 feet to the second deck that was about 8 to 10 feet off the ground. Shoes had to be taken off at the foot of the ladder. At the foot of each bunk were 5 synthetic blankets made out of peanut shell fiber and a rigid pillow in the shape of a small cylinder packed with rice husks.

Chapter 10 tanagawa pow camp

Officers and enlisted men were assigned to work parties. After sleeping under my two thin flannel blankets, I put on a double set of clothing. The work gang set off on the hike to the quarry at 8:00 a.m. and was assigned to various jobs. I ended up being one of the rock loaders into the wood box on wheeled mine carts which rode the wood rails with manpower pushing them. The rocks were used to fill in the shore line to make a big area for necessary housing material to complete the dry dock. Also, if finished, the area would be space for warehouses for materials for restoring ships, etc.

The blasted rocks were sharp and cut into our fingers if grabbed carelessly and let go of quickly. My hands were cut by broken chips until I learned to use ragged clothing cut to usable size to grab the sharp rocks. I also learned that I had to be careful not to drop them. Later, one hit my arch and sent me to my bunk for a week until I was again able to walk. The worst thing about the work was the COLD wind off the open sea. Japanese contractors used the POWs as slave labor. The guards worked for the contractor building the dry dock and were pressured to see that we worked! Their "persuaders" were "kendo sticks", rifles, or just plain kicks on the body until we got up, or were helped up by a fellow POW to hang on to the car while others pushed and unloaded it. I was hit many times with the "Kendo stick" on my neck, shoulders, back, hips, and legs even though I tried to stay clear of the very bad guards.

3 December 1942

The Japanese finally decided to help us get rid of the body lice. They authorized us to find enough wood to heat tubs of water to boil our clothing and be lice free. Our clothing was boiled, as well as the thin flannel blankets. Everything went pretty good for about two weeks, and then the lice returned. We boiled items all over the compound. When the frost formed, we knocked out the frost and took them inside. Also, as all our clothes were boiled, we ran back to our blankets in our bare skin. Nothing eliminated the lice. We just endured. The short food rations, the cold, and the rags we wore made life miserable.

By this time my hands became more toughened and I no longer used rags for gloves. My hands did feel like they were frozen, but I managed to keep from getting frost bite by putting these inside my clothing as often as possible. The camp commander told us we would be paid for our work. This did not make us work any harder than we were forced to. The sickest one was almost blind according to one of the doctors; some still had malaria. Fortunately, I had not had any recurrences since the cold weather.

A day or two later as I hiked back to camp after work, I was thinking how good it would be to get inside from the snow. I was met with news that ten POWs in the bay below me had died that morning after I had gone to work. It included my friend Lt. C. W. Wood. The camp commander and our Col. Miller requested 25 volunteers from our barracks to carry them to the crematory and I volunteered. It was a rough night; the snow was still coming down lightly, but enough to make it slippery. The dead were wrapped into their blankets and tied onto a long pole. Two POWs carried one dead POW and five extra POWs came along to cut wood. This wood was added to each dead POW's pole, which didn't make the burden any lighter. The woodcutters also would relieve the carriers. The crematory was about two miles along the beach road. I often wondered how I made it back to the barracks. Our rations were saved, but they were about half the normal amount. We complained but it did no good.

7 December 1942

We were allowed to send ONE post card and I wrote to my wife, Nell. "Your Card written 27 August 1942 was received today. I read the few sentences with joy. Other POWs received many letters but I was happy with the one from you. I gladly read the post card and found out later it was mandated by the Japanese commander. Several officers tried not to fill out one, but were made to change their minds when the commander threatened to cut food rations for those not sending cards. My diary notes on 16 December "Your birthday, sweetheart, but no presents, no card, and no greetings. I can only think of you from my memories. I had filled out a few words on a post card ten days ago, and sent you my love."

16 December 1942

The weather turned very cold and we worked shorter hours. Even the guards in their long winter coats were shivering. It froze the water pipe into camp and work parties to the quarry were postponed two days until the pipe was back in service. In our skimpy clothing it was cold and difficult work to dig the frozen dirt to find the pipe, pry it open for repair; then dig another ditch 10 to 12 inches deeper to get below the frost line. My hands and feet were frostbitten and barely escaped serious damage.

The officers were now exempt from work parties in the rock quarry; only the enlisted men went to work at the quarry today. We would now work around the camp. With the water back on, the camp kitchen was able to cook again without hauling water. We continued rebuilding some storage buildings for the Japanese camp.

20 December 1942

Date is estimated. My diary shows ten more men died of diphtheria. They possibly caught the "bug" from one of the previous group that died. I did not volunteer for this trip to the crematory. Once was enough!

25 December 1942

NO WORK TODAY! The Japanese allowed food from the first Red Cross box, with the following items allocated to FOUR men:

1 – 8 ounce can of salmon

2 ounces of salmon for each man

1 – 10 ounce can of lunch meat

2-1/8 ounces of Spam each

1 – 3 ounce can of sardines a loud discussion on the distribution.

1 – 4 ounce box of raisins
EACH MAN WATCHES as 1 raisin is doled one at a time
1 – 4 ounce box of prunes
1 cup each. The final odd prune is divided in
4 equal shares
1 – 1 ounce square of cheese cut carefully into 4 equal pieces
1 – 4 ounce can of butter crupulously divided for the last man's choice is now having first choice!
3 – hard tack biscuits)
These last 3 items divided into 4 equal portions
3 small squares chocolate) produced a final decision just short of
3 bags of tea) fisticuffs and really tested friendships!

Starving men have very short tempers when anyone tries to get the biggest share. It is humorous now, but this happened even for a few crumbs or grains of rice.

26 December 1942

My neck and face are beginning to swell. The area around my eyes is puffy and I had to see through my eyelashes. By the time I crawled into bed my whole face was puffing up. The next morning I went on sick call. My eyelids were so puffed up I was barely able to see; for a good look I had to push my lids up with my fingers. There wasn't any medicine to give me, and in any case, the doctor didn't know what I had. He guessed I had some virus, and with luck, it would go away. At least I did feel better in a couple of days as the swelling began to go down. I didn't have to use my fingers to open my eyes. The sick were on half rations; it was better to go on the work details so I received more than a half ration. More men in the hospital died, but many were one bowl of rice from death anyway.

I visited with Lt. John Kiernan. He was in terrible shape in spite of the wool garments I sewed for him out of an Army blanket so he could keep warm as there was no heat anywhere except the Japanese's kitchen. I didn't think John would last more than two weeks. He made it and I saw him again, but he died about five years after his return to the U.S.

1-12 January 1943

Night duty of two hour shifts as fire wardens was instigated by the Japanese camp commander. This was miserable duty; it was very cold and nothing to do except stay awake in our barracks and not get caught by the Japanese guard as he inspected at irregular times. When my turn was over, it was back to bed for a chance to warm up or sleep, if possible, before waking for morning "Tinko" (head count).

The Japanese commander advised our group's senior officer, Lt. Col. Miller, that on "Yasamaa" days (holidays or Sundays or no work days) that the ration would be cut in half, the same as hospital patients get. The cold, hard work and very poor food was a monotonous routine as the days passed. My facial swelling was going down and I could see a little better. Work resumed at the quarry, but it was misery to put in my eight hours loading rock and pushing the heavy carts to the edge of the fill on the bay. It was even worse blocking the wheels so we could tip the load into the bay.

I often wished we could push the whole cart into the bay.

15 or 16 January 1943

After we had our usual rice and watery soup of a few pieces of daikon radishes if we were lucky, WE RECEIVED AN ORDER TO PACK OUR BAGS AND BE READY TO MOVE! Maj. Ore, a West Point graduate, a couple of other officers, a doctor, and all of the enlisted men stayed in Tanagawa.

The rest of us walked back to the trolley line – we hobbled more than we walked. It was freezing weather. The overloaded trolley took us to the rail station in Osaka. As usual, we nearly froze on the station platform waiting for the train and for the Japanese officers and guards to join us. Huddling in groups did not seem to be any warmer. While waiting we had an air alert; the guards were very scared. A short train ride took us to the small station of Okiyama. We hiked across the town to the waterfront and another wait. The ferry showed up in an hour and took us aboard. I was so numb with cold I can't remember if I was inside or just on the deck as the ferry hauled freight.

Our destination was the Island of Shikoku and the town of Takamatsu. Another walk to the train station, another train ride. Our accommodations were not plush!

The station of Zentsuji was a short ride, four or file miles, then another hike of about a mile. We could see a tall Pagoda in the distance; it was beautiful and very tall. Local people with ox carts loaded with various farm products were headed toward the rail station. We also noted a couple of ox carts with four to six barrels on them going different directions. One man with a straw hat (coolie) wielded a long switch to control his team. These, we found out later, were called "honey wagons" in the Orient. Very interesting were the flimsy-looking homes, with carefully manicured gardens of shrubs or a little grass.

Another building was set back from the street with a tile roof and weathered marble steps, which went through a huge stone arch. This was a religious temple. Behind the high wood fence was the compound that was to be our next residence.

Chapter 10 Tanagawa POW Camp

Chapter 11
Zentsuji Prisoner of War Camp

16 January 1943

The Zentsuji compound included (I think) four to six huge two-story buildings, one huge single-story storage building with the kitchen, and several smaller buildings. Beyond the second building, which I was in, you could look through the window for the next one-half mile or so and see more of the same buildings. This was a Japanese military training base, storehouses, and was also the current headquarters of POW camps in Japan.

We were given a welcome by the officers and contract workers, known as Sea Bees, who had been captured on Wake Island and Guam. The guards took over when the sergeant ordered us to line up four feet apart and spread all our possessions on the ground for a search of forbidden items. It didn't take long as anything of value had been taken by the Japanese long ago!

Chapter 11 Zentsuji Prisoner of War Camp

The Japanese commander then welcomed us as "hostages." We were never called Prisoners of War because hostages were not bound by the Geneva Convention Rules and they could treat us however they wanted! As I remembered them, here are some of the rules:

<u>ZENTSUJI CAMP RULES</u>

Do not try to escape; you will be shot.

Must come to attention for non-coms and salute officers.

One hair cut per month.

Must sit down to smoke in buildings with ash tray near, also a can of water in which to put out the cigarette.

Shall not assemble in groups of more than ten without permission.

Do not loan, give, or gamble Yen.

Do not shake blankets.

Do not drive nails anywhere (what nails?).

Do not use vacant rooms.

Do not carry matches, drugs, knives, etc.

Do not use costumes or cosmetics, and no dancing.

Censored mail – each officer allowed to write three letters and two postcards a year.

Do not sit on bed.

Do not lie down, except with permission.

Do not use blankets during day.

Do not whistle in compound.

Do not sit on well or "Benjo" covers as it is extremely dangerous to your health if you fall in.

Do not lock Japanese office windows.

Do not sleep during day.

Must sit at attention for Japanese guards.

There are no restrictions on use of water if it is not taken from faucets. (There was no water EXCEPT in faucets!)

The Canteen (Japanese Store) is selling daily commodities of food stuffs and items for the "hostages," including dental product. (Items were ground-up black, bitter food, toothpaste, tooth brushes and playing cards!)

After we had made our required "bow," the Japanese Commander went to

his office and the Senior American Camp Officer, U.S. Navy Medical Corps, Capt. W. T. Linsberry, took charge.

We couldn't enter the barracks until we had haircuts and shaved our beards. This was done between a couple of barracks so we would have a little protection from the wind and be nearer to the bath house. RHIP (Rank has Its Privilege); the Colonels were the first to shed beard, hair, and the fat lice hiding in them. Hair and lice were very carefully collected on a big sheet; when it was full. the sheet was carefully taken and the lice and hair burned. As the men were sheared, they shed all clothes and walked to the bath house. After bathing he was given a pair of pants, shirt, and his shoes. Then the American Colonel had his helper designate the room and building where his "home" would be. It took most of the day before we lowly 2nd Lts. had our turn.

My turn came late in the afternoon. Hal Joslin, U.S. Navy, sheared my head to the skin. (This was a happy time for me as I knew Hal in Seattle when he was newly married to Marie. Years later Hal was promoted to Capt. and I would see him at our Zentsuji Reunions.

It was great to shed my clothes and go to the bath house carrying my shoes. I didn't know a Japanese bath house was one big tank of water about 25x35x4 feet deep and made of concrete. I went in and scrubbed with a big bar of strong soap. It sure felt good. An unpleasant sight was a corner of the tank where dirt, dead skin, soap suds, lice and their eggs floated in a two-inch-thick, eight-foot-wide circle of scum; but our filthy bodies had not felt this good since we had been taken prisoner. Clean clothes were issued to us; our filthy clothes were taken, boiled, dried, and returned to us a few days later. Our blankets received the same treatment.

The U.S. Navy, Marines, British Navy, Dutch Navy, Australian Army and Navy, and the New Zealand Army and Navy who were already living here loaned us clean clothing. As soon as we had bathed and dried, we put them and our shoes on, found our room and sleeping location. Our blankets were returned very promptly to our assigned room number and it was wonderful not to have lice chewing us. There was no heat in our barracks and just the thin blankets (like American cotton flannel) to keep us warm while sleeping on our wooden planks.

Each room had a leader who we referred to as our "Honshu." Each POW had his own cup and bowl for rice and vegetables and the first few days the rations were big; we ate every crumb! The earlier POW inmates took a cut so we could feel like we were alive again. The rations were evened out again the second or third day, but I really appreciated it. Our room Honsho was Robert Fulton, Lt.., U.S. Navy, from the USS HOUSTON, the heavy cruiser. The HOUSTON had been the flag ship of the U.S. Asiatic Fleet until it was sunk in the battle of the Java Sea in the Sunda Straight during the 1 March 1942, battle with the Japanese Naval Force. Lt. Fulton was normally in the engine room, but at the time of battle he had been on rotation tour of duty on the bridge. When the ship started sinking he dived overboard and swam to shore. He was captured by the Japanese on the Island of Java and shipped to Tokyo for interrogation. He was then sent to Zentsuji where he became our "Honsho" (room commander). He was responsible to the Japanese guards to see that we didn't set the building on fire and were present for morning and evening body county. The worst of his duties was to divide the rice or millet and watery vegetable soup so no one could complain! He was well liked by all of us.

January 1943

About the 23rd the Japanese camp medics gave us a shot in the arm. I'm not sure what it was for; scuttlebutt said it was for smallpox; also a cold smear for whatever it was good for – I never found out.

The days passed slowly but someone had a deck of cards to play Bridge. Not many, including me, knew how to play, but soon there were several teachers and more decks of cards. Two top players and teachers were Ensign Russell Snow and Army Lt. Martin Schechter.

Samuel Trifilo was a beginner like me when he could work it in as Sam also taught TWO of the Spanish classes. What Spanish I know today I learned to speak, read, and write in Sam's class. My memory was not too good as a cup (small tuna can size) of millet doesn't nourish the body and memory. (I did receive a B+ for advance class examination for credits when I returned to the University of Washington after the war and I went back to graduate.) Between work duties, weekends, or evenings we played or read books. I was recently reminded that I had brought the Spanish book through Bataan and Corregidor to Zentsuji. Guess the Japanese didn't think it was worth stealing, but it was quite an addition to our library.

Thanks to two smart POWs who could read the Japanese newspapers. the enlisted men would smuggle into camp from work parties in Takamatsu, the rail connection with the main island ferry. We got some news of the war. It was always six months old when the Japanese censors would allow the news to be printed for the Japanese public. When it came to battles or losses, the public was only told how many planes or ships they shot down or sunk, or U.S. lives lost. Their losses were always minimal. The Osaka newspapers were printed in English and later only in Katakana symbols. The English paper was dropped in December 1943 when the war started turning against the Japanese.

Food was a big thing for us and an improvement over anything we had received since we left Cabanatuan for Japan. Before I was captured on Corregidor I had beriberi (nutritional deficiency) swelling in my legs. Vitamin B was not found in our diet of plished rice, millet, or cracked wheat. I weighed 165 pounds before beginning to fight in Bataan; from that time until I was released from captivity I continually lost weight. It was the poor food along with the starvation rations and I suffered from every vitamin deficiency known. Navy doctors from Guam, Capt. W. T. Lineberry and Lt. Commander H. J. VanPeenan told the senior American officers who had come into Zentauji from Tanagawa with us that we were "one jump ahead of being starved beyond the point of recovery to normal and that it was doubtful if all would ever reach that point." I never did recover fully and still suffer from Avitaminosis (long term vitamin deficiency).

In spite of the small rations of food at Zentauji I gained 18 pounds from January 1943 to December 1943, 148 pounds was my heaviest in captivity and 105 pounds in August 1945 was my lowest weight. By then I was a living skeleton.

January 1943 was no better than December 1942 in Tanagawa. It was cold and snowy. It didn't take long till the guards were becoming rough about smoking in our room if we were not seated at the table and didn't have a small can with water for an ash tray. I started smoking at this time because Japanese cigarettes were available; also some cigarettes came in a Red Cross box; cigarettes helped hunger pangs. I was educated to the "seated" rule when a good swat of a "kendo" stick on my arm and head knocked me to the floor.

Our introduction to the Japanese room officer came early after arrival. "Saki Pete" and his sergeant and helpers gave us house regulations: No sitting on beds or lying down during room inspection or at morning or evening roll call. We had to stand at attention, after bowing, until inspection was complete. One day I was so sick I couldn't stand. After a couple of hits, I was pulled up by my neighbors. The blows left black bruises on my arm and back; I never forgot the "stand" rule! Saki Pete earned his reputation by being the

Chapter 11 Zentsuji prisoner of war camp

most-often drunk Japanese officer in the camp. Many times a U.S. Navy man helped him home after an evening on the town in Zentsuji.

14 February 1943

Three more of the Tanagawa group died and were sent to the local crematory. The weather is better and a Japanese newspaper was smuggled into camp. A messenger, protected by POW guards who watch for Japanese guards, reads the news. If a guard shows up at a room next to (or even two rooms away), the guards give a code and it is passed on that there is danger. The messenger hides the news until the guard is gone. This time the news was bad for Japanese and resulted in a cut of the food allowance for a few days. News was smuggled in quite regularly and we could follow Japanese advances or losses but by the time we left Zentsuji newspapers didn't print very often to save paper. They always reported the Allies with huge losses, but they seldom reported Japanese defeats.

15 February 1943

My first payday! It was for 70.83 Yen. Estimated value in America at war's end was 100 Yen equals $1.00. There were unexplained deductions and I received information I was to put it in their bank and would receive it when the war was over! If I lived! My base pay, according to a Japanese 2nd Lieutenant's pay, was 70.83 Yen every 22nd of the month, less deductions for uniforms, dishes, and board and room. Also deducted was money to be banked, and then the balance was paid directly to us, from 20 Yen to 40 Yen.

One day when talking to my stepson, Larry Richter, he asked me how I was able to write with so much detail. When I told him it was my diary, he wanted to know how I was able to keep a diary and keep it hidden from the Japanese.

I had seen other POWs keeping notes and I also kept a few notes on scraps of paper, but did not have a book to keep them in. I began to look for suitable material. I'm not sure where I acquired a tablet of notebook paper. I cut it into small pages. They were small because they would have been taken by the Japanese on their routine inspections for dangerous items; dangerous because they were notes of their treatment, physical conditions of POWs, terrible food, and inhumane treatment. Capt. L. E. (Ed) Johnson from my unit of the 194th Tk. Bn. was working on the camp library repairing books brought by survivors from Wake Island or Guam and had privileges most didn't have. Capt. Johnson helped me tie and glue the pages and then glue the shelter half canvas for a cover.

Then I sewed a small book cover with compartments to carry the book. The fastened top strap had a large diaper pen I found in a garbage pile while on grass-picking work for the rabbits. This compact book carrier was pinned into the crotch of my greenish color G.I. shorts when I traveled and when I knew there would be inspections. Most of the time when we traveled and no baths for months and were very "ripe," so the guards would poke a stick at our "luggage" as it was spread out in front of us. During inspection if only one guard was checking, I would hold small items in back of me or pass it to a buddy, who would pass it back when I had passed inspection. Even when stripped to my shorts it proved to be a good hiding place. I also hid it on a sloping support of the building roof when my bunk was on the second level, I had started the book with the idea of putting in some of the outlandish recipes only a starving man could concoct, but very quickly changed it to record monthly weight, names, and addresses of fellow POWs, mail call, etc. A bonus was pictures artist friends drew in it. The main artist was Submariner Lt. K. G. (Buck) Schacht of Burlington, Washington. (He later became an Admiral in charge of the submarine fleet in the Mediterranean.)

I also acquired a needle and thread and used it all the time. Thread was harder to keep in supply, but usually some material would show up that I could pull threads, even if I had to use it double for strength. Or a POW had some he had saved and let me use. I worked for months on my projects as material and time became available. Of course, the sewing was done between studying Spanish, playing bridge, or gambling most of the Yen paid by the Japanese, or just reading library books.

I had practiced making pajamas in Tanagawa for John Kiernan, which I'm sure saved his life when he was so ill. My next project in Zentsuji was an Army-style jacket with pleated back and slanted, outside pockets to warm your hands. The jacket was made of Army pup-tent canvas and lined with a G.I. wool blanket. It was a warm coat for the Japanese winter which I gave to Ed Johnson.

My last project was to make myself a pair of overshoe

boots. They were made out of the same material as the jacket except I made them big and used some thick cardboard in the middle of the soles to stiffen them, three layers of the G.I. blanket material, and an outer cover of Army pup-tent canvas. This was the most popular item in our building. Only small-footed people could wear shoes in them; the others had to put on two pairs of socks to have a nice fit. They were in constant demand (gratis) for doing the fire watch on our floor, but they lasted through Zentsuji and into Roku Roshi camp.

My notebook shows that we were all assigned to work detail. Work details consisted of gardening, rabbits, and chickens. I was assigned to the rabbit detail to pull food for the rabbits which involved scouring the countryside for grass or any edible weeds. We competed with the farmers' cattle that had first choice. In early spring picking was good, but later in the year it was difficult to find enough food for the rabbits. We went out only in the morning and had the afternoon off.

The Navy Chief received permission to enlarge the rabbit hutches as we had more people to gather food. The cages were built and the female rabbits were allowed to grow up and "do what comes naturally." The summer feed made the project jump and the camp was allowed rabbit soup more often than once a month. This continued for a couple of months and chow was pretty good. Then the camp commander read the weighing records, noticed we were gaining weight, and stopped our rations of rabbit. Rabbit raising stopped and our food rations were cut.

My next detail was to help build a chicken hatchery

building for chickens and eggs. The Japanese furnished the materials and the horse manure to build a warm floor for the hundreds of baby chicks. The floor was built to Japanese specifications of a clay top over manure. This was troweled and smoothed with water sprinkled over the clay-filled dirt. After drying it was a hard, warm floor. The chickens survived and grew with very few casualties. Once they reached the age of laying eggs, the Navy Chief began to have egg soup. The Japanese began taking more and more of the eggs. Then chickens began to die occasionally and the POWs could use them for soup as the Japanese would not eat anything if they had not killed it! The Japanese began to take more of the live chickens and now more and more chickens would die overnight. The Japanese caught on, sent in a wagon, and took all the chickens away. Our chow was cut again and we were down to gardening duties.

One day a group of us rested in the shade of the Zentsuji Temple, a very old and famous one. Our guard allowed us to go in, after bowing, and climb up to the top level. We could see all over the town and our camp.

22 February 1943

– and twice more while I was in Zentsuji was Inspection Day by the Japanese. We were alerted through channels that we had to clean up our rooms, have all personal items in proper places, and be prepared to salute the authority of the "Rising Sun" until we were called to attention. We watched an ox cart bring in two quarters of beef and large pails of vegetables for our meals. Our first VIPs (very important person/people) were our local Japanese doctor, his male nurses, and other aides. This was followed by our camp commander, his staff of officers, sergeants, and interpreter to make sure we were ready for the next inspection team. About 10:00 a.m. the Japanese officers from Tokyo arrived and visited all the rooms with their "hostages." We stood at attention until the procession exited our room. They looked around at the personnel, but made comments among the Japanese.

The International Red Cross then arrived, but their officers were not allowed to talk to us, nor were we allowed to communicate with them. This was made very clear to us by the camp commander and our own Senior Officers. The inspection was approved by the "Top Brass" Japanese officers of all hostage camps in Japan. We heard nothing from the Red Cross but the inspection was satisfactory to the Japanese. The gate was hardly secured before the wagon of beef and vegetables were on the way out of the gate. This routine was the same for every inspection of Red Cross personnel. Since we were not all sick and looked reasonably well, the only report to the outside world had to be good. The VIP visitors did not linger long after formalities and were soon out of the gate on their way.

Our lunch was in our rooms as soon as the carriers could make it from the galley, but instead of a feast of meat, etc., it was the usual millet or rice and watery soup of something. The Red Cross knew of the food deception but since they didn't actually "see" it, they could not report that fact.

One of our most disliked meals was bird seed millet and salt-preserved daikon tops and in the winter and spring we had it more often. The millet was about 1/8-inch in diameter with a very hard shell; it was necessary to chew long enough to get the food value out of the small amount served. Most of it went through our system without getting any benefit. I was so hungry all of the time that I just didn't chew enough that, along with the dysentery, I didn't receive any food value from it. The daikon tops were soaked in fresh water prior to cooking and cut into short pieces, but they were still very salty. A mouthful would be chewed into a wad of stringy pulp about the size of a large cherry – no food value there either. Sweet potato vines were no better unless they were picked very young. Easter was celebrated with gravy but no meat in our millet.

Gardening March 1943 to fall 1944

We spent hours digging up new garden plots and stacking the sod on one side of the field to make compost. Digging crews worked with crude shovels and clumsy hoses. They were nothing like we had in America. Preparing the sod-cleared ground was as difficult as digging the sod. No tool was sharp enough and it was all "brute strength and awkwardness." It took all our strength to keep it up for six days a week. After digging we planted the sweet potato "eyes" and our guard "Gobo" fertilized each planting with the "honey" from the barracks. Gobo was our gardening work party guard. He was not mean, but kept us busy as he really knew how the Japanese gardened and we did it his way.

One time I was with a party of workers and walked to a pottery where we loaded a couple of huge clay tanks on a rubber-tire cart. We took them to a couple of garden sites we worked on, dug a deep hole and buried the tank almost to ground level. The tanks were used for storage of the "Benjo" cart containers and used for fertilizer by Gobo. Some guards were easy-going when they were the only one, two would be very strict. Gardening was fun with one guard and he was generous with his cigarettes. The Japanese farmers kept everything neat and clean and their homes with small shrubs and flowers were well tended.

Gardening details included both morning and afternoon work for clearing the garden and planting. The gardens were to be a joint effort to be shared by the POWs and the Japanese. When we raised sweet potatoes, the Japanese got the potatoes and we got the tops; the same for daikons, we got the tops and they took the roots. The gardens were also for the Japanese civilians as they were very low in food.

2-31 April 1943

Routine work parties kept us busy, but did allow some time off as the gardens have been planted, at least the ones I'd been working on. It had warmed up quite a bit and we had some sunny days. I always looked forward to Saturday, especially after digging in the garden as sometime we would have hot water for bathing. If not, we could take a cold wash down in the "Benjo" where there was a cold water faucet.

30 May 1943

The garden work parties continued as new plots were made available for us to work on. After evening check in, the alarm came from camp headquarters that there was a shovel missing. The entire camp was called out to search for the shovel. Near the end of the first hour's search the shovel was discovered in an adjoining bin of different tools. They were all old, obsolete, very crude, and difficult with which to do anything. We were excused to go back to quarters and a cold dinner.

After one big area was planted in sweet potatoes we dug up some new graded field and planted daikons. In other areas we had pumpkins; I don't remember if we had any squash. The weeds grew prolifically with the plentiful fertilizer. Harvesting the crops in the fall was eagerly anticipated as we figured our meals would be better. Each day a heap of potatoes or daikons would be harvested and left in the field for the wagons to pick up. The heaps were always gone by the next morning, but none ever reached our compound kitchen. The same procedure was followed in 1944. The Japanese lied to us and disposed of all the produce. We were only allowed the food that Tojo and his buddies had allotted to the "hostages." No wonder we ended up skin and bones! We didn't live; we just existed by God's will.

One day on our way back to camp we caught up with a farmer's wagon loaded with tangerines on the way to market. Our lone guard led the way and didn't watch the rear. As we passed the wagon the farmer watched the guard, and then carefully motioned for us to take the tangerines. Every one marched fast enough and we loaded our pockets. By now a full pocket on our skinny bodies didn't show and cause a search. The farmer was happy to give them to us as the

Japanese Army just took his crop and did not pay for them.

Summer was the time for gardening, but we did have time to read, study, play cards, chess, or even a hair cut every month. We had church on Sunday – no work parties – and sometimes receiving mail. I had one card in 1943, 8 cards and letter in 1944, and only 1 card with a picture in 1945 (I received only 10 cards or letters and one picture from Nell during my POW days.) I loved receiving them as I had only four cards from other friends and relatives during my time as a POW.

Our time in Zentsuji was the same routine of work parties and holidays. Outages were a routine for holidays; electric outages; no water in pipes or too much rain; also snow, sometimes we had up to 8 inches; and there were days when the cold, icy wind, would delay work. The barracks were NOT heated so we wore all our clothing to try to keep warm.

We sometimes have lectures from officers who had interesting experiences. One in particular was Capt. J. C. Archer. His "Aussie" accent, Australian vocabulary, and hair-raising experiences kept the crowd enchanted and the rooms overcrowded. Capt. Archer had spent many years in Papua, New Guinea as a government ranger patrolling the area to keep peace and keep the natives concealable on health information. His escapades covered many years of traversing the high mountain tropical island and visiting many primitive native villages. In addition to bugs, snakes, and wild animals, he had to stay alert to keep headhunters (which some New Guineans were) from tossing him in their pot and displaying his head on their so-called hunting headquarters lodge. He was 6' 4-1/2" tall with a big-boned lean frame so he must have been quite impressive to the short natives. In one of his trips before he was able to stop the practice of headhunting, he was offered some smoked flesh from one of their raids. Natives had a big collection of heads at various villages. The raids were stopped, but tribes kidnapping women from other tribes continued for some years. It was rumored by soldiers fighting in the area that the mountain tribes would not let the Japanese into their area and many Japanese lost their lives trying.

5 March 1943

It was shortly after head count the guards left us, and we were waiting for our morning rice that there was a fairly strong earthquake. The guards rushed us all out into the big outdoor area and lined us up for another head count. They didn't want any casualties in case the building collapsed. The roofs were of red tile and their heavy weight really made the buildings sway. This was our first quake in Zentsuji, but there were many more, some light; others were stronger and we had to evacuate the buildings.

Guards were usually rotated every few months to duties in the Japanese Army to other areas. Three I remember well who came at different times were a Japanese guard from Spokane, one from the Puyallup Valley south of Seattle, and our last one came from Los Angeles. These individual guards were well educated and spoke English as well as we did. They were friendly when no other Japanese were around. They did not like the Japanese Army, but had to serve; and did not believe the Japanese would win the war. Most of our guards were disabled soldiers from the China campaign and later from the South Pacific. Some guards were meaner than others and would hit you or kick you, just as they had been treated by their superiors in the Japanese Army. Some were friendly when only one was with a work group but were all "business" when there were two or more as they didn't want any "report to go back to headquarters about them. We had nicknames for many: "Horse Face," "Club Fist" (artificial hand), "Peg Leg" (artificial leg), and "Leather Wrist."

Many activities were repeated daily or monthly. We went to church on Sunday, Catholic or Protestant; I usually went to Catholic services except when they had communion. The most outstanding Chaplain was the Catholic Priest, Capt. V. S. Turner. Nearly every Sunday he had a message concerning our lives as hostages and how we should conduct our lives with each other and our captors. After the war ended, he continued his work in Australia, always promoted to high office until his death in 1993.

Most months ends with paydays in Yen. We played Black Jack with it as there were only were worthless items in the Japanese canteen; one time there were playing cards but they didn't last long. I never won – it's a dealer's game. Baths were on the last Saturday – if there was enough wood to heat water. Every month there was an inspection of our rooms for clean floors and neatness. Lots of time was sent going to the "Benjo," (10-20 hole covered toilet), as our poor diet caused dysentery and diarrhea. Japanese farmers cleaned the "Benjos" in winter with their 8 or 10 barrel "honey wagons" pulled by four oxen as the waste was stored in a big crock buried in a garden corner and dipped out as needed for fertilizer for the garden. The poor Japanese farmers, in wide-brimmed straw hats, ragged shirt, knee-length pants, and sandals for shoes, dipped all the Benjos from the 3 or 4 buildings weekly. The wagon or two-wheel cart had two or 3 barrels and a couple of cows to pull it to their gardens.

One month we had a load of bean buns from the bakery next to our outside wall around the camp. The buns were filled with sweet brown beans and there was only one bun each. Another time we had a load of small doll-size baked loaves of bread, possibly from the same bakery, and each of us had one loaf. It was wonderful. The good times didn't last.

9 March 1943

The Japanese passed a box of Red Cross food and tobacco to each POW. The times crossed off the picture list and were sent to the galley for the cooks to use for soups for everyone. Trading items became very lively and tobacco was the highest priced item. I really enjoyed American cigarettes and smoking tobacco in my old pipe. A half cigarette was enough to cut my hunger and when cigarettes became scare I would cut them into thirds and get enough nicotine to make me dizzy. It cut hunger pangs enough so that I was satisfied with the chow, even when it was very short! I usually traded my coffee for cigarettes. (I still don't drink coffee!)

13 May 1943 –

AIR RAID PRACTICE.

We had to go into the buildings; the guards were more irritable than usual as we lined up for head count. This date no more newspapers were allowed into camp and food quantity and quality were cut even more. We were getting a few beans mixed into our millet; or in our watery soup, a small piece of tofu, orange, taro root, bamboo shoots, gobo (a type of spinach), daikon tops, or the real daikon root – just a few very small pieces in each cup.

We began to get afternoons off so were able to read in our "library." I had many chess games with my friend Ronald Faubel, who had been approved to train at an air base in the U.S. for the Dutch Air Corps of Java. The Japanese cancelled his plans. He stayed in the Dutch Air Force, flew military planes, and retired to the Netherlands. Willy, his wife, said that he died from serious, long term illness 31 October 1992, at age 72.

29 May 1943

The Japanese celebrated Emperor Hirohito's birthday with a 10-gun salute and a lot of loud music, singing and dancing with beautiful exotic costumes. We watched from the second floor of our barracks until the camp commander posted guards and cleared the floor until the ceremony ended.

Chapter 11 Zentsuji Prisoner of War Camp

1 June 1943

As with our first Red Cross box, we traded very little and hoarded the rest as we didn't know if we would ever receive another. We did a trade in rice by holding a one-half portion of rice and trading the rest to another willing POW. The "loaned" rice could be called in on a certain day and provide a big ration that could be enhanced by using a hoarded item from the Red Cross box. I traded and called in my "trades" when I wanted to celebrate a special date, like an anniversary of marriage or birthday. As the rations became smaller, there was less trading as we needed every morsel.

I was lucky to have gone to Zentsuji Camp as this was the biggest and the "show" camp for Tojo's brass to show the Red Cross and the camp with the highest rank of POWs from the countries fighting the Japanese. The Red Cross, to my knowledge, did not go to the ordinary "slave" camps where the prisoners worked in underground mines, coal mines, copper mines, manufacturing plants and steel mills – all for the Japanese war machines.

The summer sun was really hot. Many times we had to take off all but our shorts (if we had any) to work. Many POWs used a "G-string" which consisted of a string around the waist and a piece of cloth (about the size of a half pillow case) to go from the back, down between your legs, and up the front and over the top of the string; the excess length dropped down toward your knees. I tried this once but I burned and blistered so finally suffered with a pair of pants and some kind of short-sleeve shirt. Mosquitoes and flies were everywhere and we really got chewed!

20 June 1943

Many times after a day's work, back in my barracks, I noticed my legs were swollen; they would cramp and ache. Malaria also hit me a couple of times that summer. Sick call helped me get over the malaria as I could lie around until it wore off. My weight varied with diet, but not any big changes – I was just plain skinny.

One Sunday Capt. D. C. Hutchinson-Smith of Wahroonga, Sydney, Australia, and Lt. Arnie Carlson, U.S.A., and I sat down on a plank lid over a big tank – a "no no" and our gab fest was promptly cut off by a visit to the camp commander's office. Our punishment was to stand at attention for an hour. Lt. Nakajini, our Japanese room officer (we called him Sake Pete because he was so drunk most times) made us read ALOUD the camp rules and promise not to sit on a plank lid again. The guards slapped each of us a couple of times and let us go.

Christmas 1943

With Japanese permission, we talented producers found enough musical instruments among the earlier captives to have a good band, which also lead to some really great carol singing. Our show maestro produced the famous Dickens "A Christmas Carol: complete with costumes for all the famous characters: Scrooge, Bob Cratchett, Tiny Tim, and including Mrs. Cratchett played by me! The play was very successful, even when Mrs. Cratchett lost one of her breasts and could not replace it. The evening ended with us singing many other carols, fun songs, and military numbers. A full house, including the camp commander and his staff, enjoyed it.

Chapter 12
The Year 1944...

It was boring as far as our activities were concerned. Food was cut again as the "Tanagawa" group, of which I was a member had gained a little weight. This year I averaged a weight loss of 2.3 kilos every month and weighed in at 115 pounds in November; the so-called soup of hot water, pieces of daikon, cucumber, sweet potato vines, etc. was definitely not nourishing. My trips to the "Benjo" increased due to dysentery and got even worse when the weather turned cooler. Frequently, especially at night, my legs would swell and cramp. If I bent over to pick up something I would black out if I rose up too quickly or from any sudden movement. My energy was rapidly dwindling.

Fire drills came at surprising times and we really had to be on our toes so everything "was up to snuff." Ashtrays had to have water in the bottom, not too full; always ready for use.

Chapter 12 The Year 1944 ...

Smoking was allowed only around the table.

Air raid drills began this year and were held more often as the year progressed. It must have had something to do with activity of American planes!

About the middle of summer the camp commander announced we could dig up around the compound's board wall to make gardens to increase our food supply. The soil was rich, not too wet, and easy to dig down deep. The POWs started planning. I don't know who the "mastermind" was, but believe all shared. The "gang" was all from my room #27. They figured out how to get into the Japanese Army warehouse to find food, and they knew they could crawl under the fence. A signal system was worked out to avoid guards and get back safely.

Night raiders would dig under the camp wood fence, crawl under in the dark, and go to nearby Japanese storage buildings, push up the floor plank, and go in to steal rice, sugar, millet, anything they could find to eat. The room #25 bandits: Lt. Sam Dillard III, Lt. Gayle Hilley, Lt. John Noles, all three fly boys; Lt. Wayne Hightower, Signal Corps; and Emil Michaick, Ordinance. I think the last regular bandito was in the regular crew. They would pick a dark night and two would stand watch to signal danger if a Japanese was likely to see them. The other two would dig into the soft dirt, crawl under, fill their sacks or other items with whatever they could, being careful to turn sack's opening away from casual view. They would carefully replace the loose board in the floor, and then toss a small rock over the fence to hit the toilet walk or roof. If all clear, one pebble would be thrown back. The "thieves" would slip home to Room #27. They would take a chair and one would help the other lift the food through a trap door to the attic. The food was stored, cooked immediately, or held until they wanted to cook a feast for their gang. Their stove was electric made up of many pieces collected over a period of 6 months or so from the Japanese junk pile. I almost joined them when Hilley asked if I would be a guard and signal. They were waiting for a favorable night to go and I said "yes." Gayle's party never did go outside again.

A raiding crew from the next barracks was caught by one of the Japanese night guards as they returned. They were sentenced to spending a week in the wood prison with bars of 2x4s and limited to a small room where it was impossible to stand or sit. The building was locked with a heavy wood door and was cold at night and sticky hot and sultry during the day. The mosquitoes were terrible and they were allowed NO clothing, real starvation rations, and no water. When they were released they had been almost eaten alive and were too weak to walk.

Chapter 12 The Year 1944 ...

Chapter 13
1944 and 1945

Newspapers were discontinued leading to wild rumors. They were never able to completely stop newspapers as somehow they were smuggled into the compound. These were carefully scanned by our two officers (who read and spoke Japanese), and who then would write a brief news report and were sent to all POWs' rooms, which were then burned in the cook fires. Some of the POWs kept a chart of the Japanese's advances or retreats as published, even though the news was from three to six months old by the time we saw them. Most of it was good from the Japanese point of view. Any retreats made by the Japanese were not printed and the public had to believe Tojo and company. Most of the Japanese public did not know of the thousands of us in POW camps in their country.

The Japanese commander began to tighten up inspections.

Chapter 13 1944 and 1945

The surprise inspections included searching pillow cases and our so-called mattresses, which were made out of cut-up pieces of twisted vegetable material (possibly rice straw); and went through our sacks of belongings – anything personal-looking for anything that had been stolen or something that could be made into a weapon were taken.

They also cut our food rations again. Hunger has been my constant companion ever since I was shot in the neck while fighting in Bataan. Japanese rations constantly got worse, never better, so when we did get a Red Cross food packet, it was necessary to ration the contents. (We could have finished a box in two days!) By saving and trading millet we could have one fairly good meal occasionally. Some get-togethers were: the first was when Sam Trifilo and I celebrated Thanksgiving in August 1944. We considered this to be the first full meal in months. On other occasions I traded and had meals with Hal C. Seymore, and others. These meetings were called "Quaking" and were often to celebrate something, such as when Hal Joslin and I received mail in August 1944 that my wife Nell and his wife Marie had finally gotten together to visit. (We were married the same month in Seattle and had met one night at a dance at Fort Lewis about a week before we went our way to war; Hal with the Navy and I with the Army.) Even though I was starving I saved something from the Red Cross box and celebrated Nell's and my anniversary and every birthday by quaning. (That is why the News Bulletin put out by the American Defenders of Bataan and Corregidor (ABCD) is called THE QUAN.

22 December 1944

– was an eventful day. It was cold and, as usual, no heat in our building. I bundled up with all my clothing to try to keep warm. My big, homemade boot shoes came in handy with a pair of cotton socks to wear. We received a Red Cross box for Christmas, but ten of us had to share the contents. Even the smallest amount was wonderful and appreciated.

Christmas Eve we had a big attendance for an evening of singing Christmas carols, then off to bed as soon as we had "count off" and lights were out.

29 December 1944

There was a very heavy distribution of mail which cheered everyone. I received two post cards from Nell and felt better that I was not completely forgotten. Some POWs received up to 15 letters!

The main topic of daily discussions was FOOD, FOOD, and MORE FOOD, and then the war. There were air raid alerts and many more alarms.

27 January 1945

My notes said "Phew, I finally had a Quan party! Something didn't agree with me and the "Benjo" runs got me!

The Japanese came up with new instructions for air raids: "Pull all curtains and second floor POWs go to first floor and line up for "Tinko" (head count), When the "all clear" is given we may resume activities.

I went to the so-called dental office with an excruciating pain but they were no help as there was no material for

Chapter 13 1944 and 1945

cavities. The next day I went back and had the doctor pull my wisdom tooth without pain killer medication. It really hurt but it was better than the ache.

Weather is very cold now. My hands, feet, and legs have finally had prickly pains at times. Many others have the same problems. Some found a wash pan, filled it with cold water, and put their feet into the water until the feet were without feeling. Then they slept until the feet began to warm, then would repeat the operation.

18 February 1945

This was a disappointing day for me. About four bags of mail came in; 3,000 or so letters. Most POWs received ten or more letters or cards, some only three or four, but I received none. My turn came in March when I received my last mail from Nell, a letter with a picture; it sure helped my morale.

17 March 1945

The month is full of air raids. We heard bombs one evening. The Japanese began blackouts during air raids. The food is becoming even skimpier and now we feast on salt pickled daikon tops with their woody stems and leaves. We chew and spit out a pile of wood. Millet has been cut 10%; no wonder we are hungry and all we think of is food. At last the weather is starting to warm up a little. Hal Joslin had to go back to work after a bad case of chilblains. (Chilblains is a medical condition often confused with trench foot and frostbite. It can be reduced to keeping hands and feet warm in extremely cold weather.)

April 1945

More air raid alerts and lots of rumors. Someone thought they saw a B-29 one evening. We heard President Roosevelt had died and the chaplains held a short memorial service. Food has hit bottom but work parties continue. I am losing weight and strength. There are many rumors of Zentauji breaking up and moving out!

10 May 1945

We received a Red Cross box but all the items like cheese, sardines, corned beef, Spam, or dehydrated soup were taken out to help the kitchen feed the working parties, and we officers were allowed some of the rest. The balance of EACH box was split among TEN men. (See page 64 for a list of what each box contained.) By now all of us have swollen legs due to poor diet.

Rumors are still flying that we will be moved. The officer's work parties are still on. Later, the same day, the move was confirmed but not the destination. We heard that Germany was out of the war on 5 May 1945. We are all very tense. I can't concentrate on studying my Spanish lessons. Work parties, reading, playing bridge, and guessing games help pass the time.

28 May 1945

Another Red Cross box received and the procedure was the same: ten men share after the kitchen takes theirs. Little did we know that this was the last Red Cross box we would ever receive. Trading of rice and millet was on again and the "coffee parties" with Hal Joslin and John Kiernan were on again. They brought their own coffee.

<u>10 June 1945</u>

The pending move of the American Officers was postponed to the 13th of June: destination Fukui Prefecture, northwest of Osaka. The air activity has increased with many more sirens sounding off. The crews working at Takamatsu picked up information that the air raids were damaging the big cities and the rail tracks.

The warm weather is here and so are the bugs and flies. The flies are a real nuisance and the bed bugs and fleas are eating us!

Chapter 14
Roku Roshi

<u>*24 June 1945*</u>

Information came to us early that this was moving day. My bags had been packed the night before and the bedding had been stuffed into the bag before morning chow. I knew the general area we were heading, but without a map it was hard to picture the paradise we all hoped for. Last night we had talked, and talked, and got very little sleep.

We hiked to the rail station in Zentsuji and rode to Takamatsu where we waited for the ferry. The ferry came about 10:00 a.m. and we sailed across the choppy Pacific Ocean to Okayama. The group of 350 men was made up of all American officers from the Army, Navy, and Marines. We were met at the dock by guards who marched us to the train depot, a huge building with a big dome where we were to sit down and spend the night. I think we had a typical Japanese traveler's dinner from a Binto box. The concrete floor was not as soft as the bed I left in Zentsuji, but NO flies or bedbugs.

By night the air raid sirens were howling and the guards were really patrolling the big room we were in as they were afraid we would try to leave. The American planes (B-29s) must have had a bigger target than our depot as we never did hear the planes. In the morning we had our Binto box breakfast of rice, pickled daikon, some seaweed, a tangerine, and a couple of chopsticks. The tangerine was really enjoyed; even the skin was eaten.

The next train from the south stopped about mid-morning and we loaded for the next destination. The guards made us pull down the shades, but as soon as they turned their backs we would peek out. Before long the train slowed and we traveled over a long section of track and saw the bombed areas of Kobe and Osaka. We were unloaded in Osaka and taken to a section of the city that had some shelter under which we sat. The guards surrounded us as we waited for the next train. While we waited the Japanese public gathered around us to see what we looked like. Some of the women were very beautiful in their colorful traditional Japanese dresses with cummerbunds; some of the men were well dressed. But most were poor and appeared to be laborers.

After about three hours the train came creeping into the station; they were late because they had to wait for repairs to bomb-damaged rails. They hurriedly loaded us to try to get away before any more bombers came. They again pulled down the shades, but we managed to peek out enough to see where the bombs had fallen and buildings were destroyed.

After some very rough track (it felt like our train might tip over) we turned onto another set of tracks, these were OK and smooth; we headed west and up over some high hills. We saw Lake Biwa and rural farming and green countryside while we had our last Binto box. The next stop was Fukui and we left the train.

Fukui was a big city and had not been bombed. We waited for the trolleys that would take us out of the city. We did not know where we were going, but we were now in low land farming country. At last the trolley stopped and we got off in an area that had trees all around. It was about 7:00 p.m. and almost dark, but we were not given the time to look around as the guards were anxious to start our hike up the big hill and the narrow trail zigzagged. There was a guard in the lead with others interspersed throughout the column; I was somewhere in the middle. It was about a four-mile hike uphill and the guards tried to set a fast pace. There was a light rain most of the way and many places on the trail were wet and very slippery. It was also very steep in many places. I fell a few times, as did many others; it was dark and what moonlight there was between showers was hidden by the trees. The "hill" turned out to be a considerably high mountain. We were getting very tired, but the guards tried to not push us harder than we were able. We were all soaked when we arrived at a big barn-like building about 4:00 a.m. after our hike of 4-5 miles and up to an elevation of 5,500 feet.

Roku Roshi was an old abandoned Japanese Army Artillery Army base located on the mountain at about 5,500 feet with a confirmed depth of 4 to 6 feet of snow during the winter.

Chapter 14 Roku Roshi

Our American Colonel decided that we would bunk in rooms by rank, so we 2nd Lts. had one section. Sam Trifilo and I decided we would take an upper bunk as if it got cold we would be a little warmer higher up.

We miserable skeletons didn't need any urging to lie down as soon as we found our bunks. The guards told us there was very little room in which to dry our wet clothes. There was no heat or fires allowed in the building as the Japanese were very afraid of fires.

In the morning we had breakfast: a cup of millet and a watery wild rhubarb soup. Grumbling was rampant, but stopped when we had to "fall out" for Tinko on the so-called parade ground between the two huge barracks. In the middle of the small area was a huge boulder about nine feet high and about 25-30 feet in diameter.

The Roku Roshi camp commander welcomed us with the usual long harangue about the glories of Japan and how they were going to win the war. The United States had forced the country to go to war because of U.S. boycotts of goods shipped from the U.S.A., the Philippines, etc. Finally, he ended with a Bonsai, which we were also required to do. Then the guards were instructed to give us the regular shakedown and take what they found to his office.

The Japanese must have thought we were dumb; after all the shakedowns we had been through that we would bring anything with us that the Japanese might want. We had hidden all the things they would take, such as diaries, notebooks, razors, mirrors, etc. in the barracks, and brought only things as our dirty clothes, socks, etc. After inspection

I picked up my bag and went back to the barracks for lunch.

It wasn't long before the Japanese guard collected our Senior Officers for a conference. It ended up that all officers were ordered to join work parties and only the bedridden would be excused. Also, the Senior Officers were to be responsible for night fire guard duty. This meant from dark to sunup two men had to be on duty at all times. All but the Senior Officers took their turns but, fortunately; there were lots of men to split the duty.

<u>26 June – 15 July 1944</u>

The next morning the garden parties were formed and we were sent about a mile around the hill behind the camp to clear brush off the side of the mountain. Some dug the brush with a clumsy mattock type of hand tool instrument, others carried it downhill below our trail and piled it up, and others fed the brush to a fire. Another group worked digging up the dirt and rocks to make the ground ready to plant. I was rotated and worked in all of the jobs.

While digging the soil for planting it was possible to find a wild root called Yama-imo (similar to the Chinese sweet potato) that could be roasted in the fire and give us a little extra food. It was a stringy kind of plant similar to a sweet potato; not very tasty, but by chewing the pulp you could get some food value. The woody strings I would spit out as they were totally indigestible.

Other food items we scavenged from our land clearing were snakes, and sometimes, a frog. These were roasted in the fire. We worked steadily, even when it rained, until the

Chapter 14 Roku Roshi

hillside was planted with sweet potatoes. This project lasted most of July. I was lucky and helped kill a fairly large snake that was roasted and divided among some close friends. Once the sweet potatoes were planted I also took my turn at carrying water for the plants.

The next project was clearing a garden area near camp which was on near level ground. The same old work left me drained of energy and I would fall down and have to rest before I could get up to continue work. If I got up too quickly I would black out and fall again. There were many guards and their orders were to "take a rifle butt" to loafers. I quickly learned to get up slowly so I wouldn't black out and have an eager guard hit me with a rifle butt.

Some men found snails and roasted them. Two POWs, Lt. Teske and Lt. John Noles, ate some red berries and paid a severe penalty. We helped them back to the barracks where they threw up for a few days and were advised by one of the Navy doctors: "Don't eat anything that you don't know for sure is good!"

Some Japanese general and staff visited our camp one morning, checked the kitchen, and found our lunch soup weeds on the table as the food gathering party had arrived just before the VIP inspectors. The Japanese guards told us the weeds were "Fuki, Galosh, and wild rhubarb." After visiting the barracks the VIPs left. The camp commander reported to our Senior Officers that there would be no changes in our diet until we harvested our food crop. In other words, there would be no change; we knew from previous years that the Japanese would take all our garden produce!

26 July 1945

Our Senior Officers had a conference with the camp commander and the results were that the Americans would take over the kitchen. I volunteered. Rice was gone and only millet and swamp weeds were on the menu. The Japanese refused to allocate any more food to the POWs.

My diary shows: "A few days ago the city of Fukui was bombed and we can see the big fire from our mountain." I was on fire patrol that night with Lt. Dale Hinton, a Navy pilot from Long Beach, California. (He was captured when he was on a mission from his aircraft carrier, ran out of gasoline, and landed on a Japanese island.) The planes were circling over our camp, one after another and heading on 'glide' for the city and dropping their bombs. Dale carefully listened to the motor sounds of the planes he had flown before he was downed. The planes circled about 5 or 6 rounds in the half hour before they went back to their carrier. No Japanese planes were heard: He knew the U.S. was doing their job and was so happy he just jumped up and ran inside to tell his Navy buddies about the activity. Two lonely fire watchers now had half of the camp watching the sky become brighter every time the planes dropped more bombs. The fires raged and big columns of smoke filled the sky. Our morale grew by leaps and bounds. Everyone was cheering. I was surprised but the guards didn't do anything to stop us. We went back into the building, some to sleep, others to talk. By the time I went off fire guard duty the kitchen crew (including me) were on their way to start the fires and begin preparations to cook breakfast.

Chapter 14 Roku Roshi

Camp routine remained the same. My kitchen duties were to feed the fire and wash pots. It was better than the garden work parties or going out to pick swamp weeds for our soup. My diarrhea has never let up in the past months and even light chores left me exhausted; I took every break I could. About this time Lt. J. I. Mallette died. He was eventually buried in Linn Co., Mississippi. He was one of the good bridge players, a bunk mate, and a very good friend. Dr. Van Peenan said it was from malnutrition and tuberculosis.

I haven't mentioned much about our biting pests: the fleas. They were in our barracks in huge quantities when we arrived. When the 0eather warmed up, so did the fleas; and they could not be controlled. They made sleeping miserable with their bites. Even the unused barracks across the parade ground had billions of fleas that were jumping so thick that they hit each other!

5 August 1945

Lts. Sam Dillard and Traves Smith sneaked out of the barracks, under the fence, and off the mountain for freedom tonight. Some school children turned them in and they were brought back to camp the next day. They were probably beaten before they were returned to camp where they were each tied to a separate post without food or water.

6 August 1945

We were kicked out of the kitchen – the Japanese would serve the chow – group punishment was meted out. Everyone was confined to barracks, night guard was doubled, and no work, no games played, no lying down, and the food was cut that day. No contact was allowed with the two escapees.

7 August 1945

It was back to work as usual today. The two escaped POWs were taken away while we were at work and no one knew what happened. (After the war was over we found out from Sam that they had been sentenced to death and taken to Osaka POW camp. They were sentenced to hard labor until the death sentence was carried out, but the Japanese surrender saved them and Sam and Traves took over the POW camp. The Japanese officers were put to work getting food for the POWs, did the serving, and everything the POWs had done for so long. They lived in a style they enjoyed. I met Sam Dillard at a POW Reunion quite a few years ago and he told me about this. Sam was a friendly pilot and had the bunk across the room from me in Zenjsuji and was a good friend. The last I heard he became a dentist in Savannah, Georgia.

Many rumors were now being started by the guards. Their morale is very low and they didn't haze us like they usually did. They only kept busy keeping us working when the camp commander came around. The guards told us there were many bombing raids on the towns. Weather was hot; we were getting weaker, and the fleas seemed to be getting stronger! Nearly everyone would black out if we moved too fast getting up. My weight was now down to 105 pounds.

Chapter 14 Roku Roshi

Chapter 15
Japan Surrenders

15 August 1945

We knew something bad must have happened to the Japanese as they were really sad when we got up this morning. As soon as we ate our breakfast (only a few minutes), we picked up the buckets and a few long-handled big cups for dipping down and lifting out the contents of the "Benjo" into the buckets to fertilize the new sweet potato plants. We had lots of equipment so all of the POWs were able to help contribute to a bountiful crop. It was a long day and we were happy to get back to the barracks.

16 August 1945

The next morning at time for "work call" the camp commander announced NO WORK TODAY on "Benjo" buckets, just normal garden work. That was a relief as no one enjoyed the stinky "Benjo" work. We heard rumors galore, but so far only wishful thinking. Some thought the war was over, but we had no way of knowing and no newspapers were available.

17 August 1945

All work parties stopped, but guards were still around to see that we didn't take off. Rumors of peace spread, but no change in our 290 grams of millet and hot water drink of soup and weeds. We sat around talking, playing cards, or just loafing ON our beds and scratched at fleas. The camp commander said orders came from the POW Headquarters in Osaka to stop all work. The 290 grams of millet was also cancelled, but we saw no difference in our diet.

21 August 1945

My diary noted that it was my fourth wedding anniversary. I thought of my wife Nell and wondered what she was doing as there had been no more mail. I had hoped to be home a lot sooner. Here I was sitting in Roku Roshi in a miserable old barracks full of fleas and slowly being starved and worked to death.

The American Camp Commander, Col. Unruh was advised that "rumors of peace" were being discussed. (Col. Unruh, U.S. Air Corps, had been released from Ofuna – Tokyo prison where the Japanese interrogated the high "brass" some time before we left Zentsuji.).

22 August 1945

A conference with the Japanese Commander by Col. Unruh, Capt. Lineberry, U.S.N., and other colonels (Australian, British, Dutch, New Zealand revealed that 'THE WAR WAS OVER!" They returned to our barracks with huge smiles on their faces and the whole barracks shook with shouts of joy and much talking into all hours of the night.   (My second wife, Caroline, advises me that she celebrated "V-J" Day (Victory over Japan) on the streets of Bismarck, North Dakota 14 August 1945, as the day Japan "sent up the white flag of surrender." The Japanese really made us wait a long time!

The Japanese were not allowed to run the kitchen, but the increase in millet didn't help us. The extra millet (hard to digest) just gave us more sour stomachs, gas pains, and more trips to the Benjo. Col. Unruh, Capt. Lineberry and others made a trip to Fukui to use a phone to call American Commanders or anyone who could help get food and transportation to our camp. They found out food would be dropped as soon as they could find us, and that we would be moving out by the 5th of September, at least.

Some of our camp members found two guards who went with them to find food for the camp. They had a nice walk to the north (the only way to go as our camp was at the end of the road). They visited a shrine along the way, but there was no rice or vegetables. The local people were bad off, too. They did get a few green pears and a few unripe grapes AND a big keg of green sake. Those that drank the sake were later sick, also with severe headaches that took the whole next day to clear. I did not drink any, but friend Byron Heichel paid the penalty.

31 August 1945

PAY DAY! The Japanese commander had the records and paid us for our work from 1 January 1943 to August 1945, less monthly deductions of various amounts. For 2nd Lts. it was Y70.83, less board and room deductions of around Y27.00 a month. I received the bank balance of Y275.96. I kept one of the bills and turned the balance into a U.S. bank on my return home. As I now remember, it received $4.00 or $5.00 for it – two years and seven months of work!

Some POWs and I took a walk north along the camp road to see the closer sights and found a beautiful Buddhist Shrine. We were invited in to see it; they had many beautiful items, my first time to see anything like this. Before we returned to the barracks we toured the small village of Roku Roshi for a couple of hours. The people were friendly, but we couldn't talk with them as we knew only a few words of Japanese. We saw the crematory overlooking the big valley below and the many rice terraces.

Last evening Capt. Linsberry, Col. Unruh, Lt. Jack Ryder, Lt. Gus Johnson of the U.S. Navy, made their way to Kyoto to attend a Red Cross meeting. They returned 1 September with all the surplus food items they could carry. Volunteers worked to 1:30 a.m. preparing all the food, woke up ALL the "sleepy heads" and we had a big feast before going back to sleep.

Chapter 16
Freedom at last

<u>*2 September 1945*</u>

THE DAY OF JAPAN'S OFFICIAL SURRENDER! I think it was late in the morning when we were visited by five B-29s. One of them made a circle outside our camp and then came in low towards the small parade ground with the big rock in the middle. We all lined up along the compound fence, the first plane opened its bay to drop the food; it looked so big we thought the food would drop on us along the fence. It looked the same to the POWs on the flea barracks side, so we changed sides. Looking back, it was hilarious to see the exchange, as each side was sure what it had done to save our lives when the drop was made.

The parade field had been cleared just in time for the drop to be made, each with its own parachute. It was a low drop, so some of the chutes didn't always open enough to soften the drop.

Chapter 16 Freedom at last

The first slow chute had a load of large tins of canned peaches. When the load hit the big rock, several large cans of peaches split open and sprayed the ground with peach halves. I had lots of company when I picked up the peaches from the ground, wiped the dirt off the peaches with my fingers and enjoyed every bite! I saw another B-29 approaching for a drop but I didn't quit eating peaches. There were lots of POWs around the big rock who were also eating canned peaches so the plane continued beyond and dropped its load on the potato patch and the brush beyond. The B-29 pilot had the good sense to drop his load away from the crazy, hungry POWs.

The planes began dropping big barrels, but a lot of the chutes failed to open fast enough to slow down the barrel. They contained dry powder items such as sugar, cereal, flour, cocoa, etc. After a lot of peaches from the broken cans had been eaten, I went down to the other side of my barracks and saw a barrel that had hit a rock; the wooden top and bottom had dropped out when the sides had caved in. One end had raw cocoa and the other end granulated sugar. I would take a handful of cocoa and then a handful of sugar; I did this several times until my stomach was extended. I topped it all off with several different candy bars. Then I headed for the water faucet. I was sick all night, but had lots of company rushing to the "Benjo." We had had no sugar, chocolate, or fruit in our diet for so long that my system just couldn't handle it. I didn't eat the delicious dinner the cooks prepared that night, but by afternoon I was eating okay and didn't skip any more meals.

In addition to food, we also received a few items of

clothing; some POWs got a whole new outfit.

One of the lieutenants knew enough Japanese to talk with a farm family and found out from his visit with them they were very poor, had only rags to wear, and very little food. About six of us gathered up all the wool garments, blankets, etc., that any POW wanted to give away. I gave them my half worn boots, a pair of wool socks, a pair of gloves I had made, and some wool blankets. We also brought soap to them as they had had no soap for a year! The six of us had an ARMFUL EACH and the Japanese were the happiest people I saw before leaving Roku Roshi. Our interpreter told us the farmer said the Japanese Government had confiscated all their produce for the war effort. The farmer did not like Tojo and his cabinet (they did not blame Empower Hirohito) as the war made him a pauper as he only had his hillside farm to support his family. The whole valley had suffered and lost their sons. The farmer's wife said all the things we brought would be cut up to make clothing and some would be for blankets to sleep on and to keep warm as the snow in winter would be as high as the wife's head! They then apologized with tears in their eyes for not being able to offer us anything except tea and thanks. Their two children were just as thankful. We thanked them for the tea and walked away with a very happy feeling.

I volunteered to help in the kitchen again, but all I did was stir some soup, wash the pots, and sometimes feed the fire with wood. There were lots of volunteers so I left to look around and listen to rumors of when we would be able to leave Roku Roshi. We had good food, wanted

Chapter 16 Freedom at last

out of our miserable barracks, be able to really clean up, and go home!

6 September 1945

Lt. Ole Johnson arrived at our camp from Fukui. He talked with our camp commanders and took Maj. "Bill" Orr with him to find out how we were to get home. Maj. Orr found out we would soon have an official team to aid our rescue.

8 September 1945

The rescue team arrived this morning and Dr. C. W. Phillips, U.S. Army, of Seattle, Washington, greeted us. He brought with him Photographer Sgt. Glen Brock of Tennessee and two women (nurses or WACs) were with him. The two women were cute and a sight for sore eyes; they were completely surrounded by POWs all the while they were in camp. The team left for the night as they did not want to sleep in our flea-infested barracks.

9 September 1945

This morning my friend Sam Trifilio and I (I'm sure the whole camp) were up early for breakfast. The colonel gave the orders to load as soon as breakfast was over as the trucks should show up anytime. By 10:30 a.m. we were all on the Japanese trucks which had low sideboards and low tailgates. We sat on our bags to pad our behinds as we bounced over the potholes in the gravel road. At the town of Ono we unloaded and waited for the trolleys to take us to Fukui to catch a train.

It was interesting to see the valley with the farmers' homes, mostly covered with straw or similar roofing; the side walls had dried daikons hanging, or new daikons or onions drying. We went through several villages and I was surprised at how long it took us to get to Fukui. The train station had disappeared, as had the city as far as we could see, except for two concrete buildings which were the city's offices and the police station. Another building left standing about a quarter of a mile away was the hospital.

As soon as we were all out of the trucks, we piled our bags along the train track. It was to be a long wait for the train so we took off to do a little sightseeing. We saw no one, only black ashes as far as we could see. The train tracks were uneven when you looked down them; the result of the July 26th bombing from a Navy carrier.

Out of curiosity, several of us walked over to the city building and looked into the first floor room to see what damage had been done. It looked okay, but in one corner was a pile of Japanese swords. Three or four POWs took one, so I did too and put it in my bag of junk, which hid it quite well. Capts. Ferris Spore, John Muir, and Ed Johnson asked me to get them one also but as soon as Col. Miller saw his officers with a sword he made them return the swords, but not everyone obeyed. Mine is now hanging on the wall in my home as a souvenir of my POW days.

The wait for the train was over five hours so we appreciated the Japanese Red Cross ladies who had a little stand for tea. I had a cup of tea and said "Arigato" which is thank you in Japanese. Finally, the train came very slowly over the

Chapter 16 Freedom at last

newly-repaired tracks. At 6:30 p.m. the conductor waved to us to board the train, using a metal step stool to get up into a car. When one car was full the next car was used. It wasn't long before we heard a "toot toot" and we were on our way to Osaka, retracing our route of June 1945. The train pulled out as slowly as it came in, the cars were tipped first one way and then the other side due to the uneven tracks.

We traveled all night on a good track, but were switched to rough railroad tracks in Osaka. Our destination, according to one of the conductors, was Yokohama. The train wobbled back and forth as much as it did in Fukui. I was looking out of the window to see the city of Osaka. It was mostly miles and miles of ashes that were sprinkled with twisted steel and humps of burned equipment from former factories. After leaving Osaka, there were a few big burned buildings, but no activity except in the countryside. There were the usual scattered farm homes as we saw before. Our train wobbled as much going into Yokohama as it had going into Osaka. The bombing had taken is toll here also.

When we unloaded in Yokohama there was a band playing and Gen. Eichelberger shook hands with ALL of us. We were guided to the row of G.I. trucks waiting to take us to the pier. As each truck was filled it would take off. At the pier a couple of Army personnel helped us unload so we didn't fall and the most beautiful guides (nurses and WAVES) sent us to the chow line.

After eating all I could, I was sent to be deloused at a plywood 3-sided building with a top. Here, after pulling my shirt open, a Navy Corpsman poked a nozzle with a release handle shot DDT down my back. He worked fast and accidentally, I think, hit the top of my head. Then he opened the front of my shirt and gave another squirt; so much came out that it lay in heaps along my belt line. Next was a good squirt in the front and back of my pants. There was so much powder that later I poured some out of my shoes! I didn't know what it was for as I had never heard of DDT. Then to the showers where a doctor checked me out and wrote down my name.

After dressing in my CLEAN new clothes, I was sent to the Hospital Ship FH-1 Tryon where I was escorted to my bunk for the trip to Manila. I was now free to roam the ship and help myself to the coffee with sugar and evaporated milk that was on all decks.

At first I just took a little coffee, and then filled the rest of the cup with milk. The next time I just filled the cup with milk; finally I would take the whole can, punch two holes in the top, take it around the corner of the deck and drink it all. It slowed my appetite a little, but I never missed a meal aboard ship! I checked later and found out I was gaining a pound a day on the ship.

12 September 1945

At 7:00 a.m. the ship sailed for Manila. I was just about walking on air as I visited the deck and made new friends, Dr. Philllips of Seattle and Sgt. Brock of Tennessee. I also got reacquainted with Sgt. Tex Simmons, 194th Tk. Bn., who had been the Chef for the Officers Mess when I first came to Fort Lewis. I didn't see much of him during the Philippine

Chapter 16 Freedom at last

fighting and lost track of him when the surrender came.

Lt. Ralph Duby, Recreation Officer for the 194th also showed up. Before the war he had arranged an especially enjoyable trip for five of us to Pagsanjan Falls about 30 miles from Manila. It is a beautiful 200' deep canyon with ferns and lush tropical plants. Two natives paddled their wood canoes up the river to the falls at the end of the canoe. The river was high and the ride downstream was as exciting as my Indian dugout canoe solo ride across the Cowlitz River when I was 10 or 11 years old.

The Tryon was cozy and comfortable, even if it was crowded, and the meals were super good. After my three and a half years of starvation it was heaven! I was happy as a kid with his first ice cream cone. The beds even had white sheets, no bed bugs, fleas, or body lice to scratch. It was wonderful!

The "cruise" from Yokohama was six days of fun, even though I saw only the Pacific Ocean and the South China Sea until we entered Manila Bay. Bataan Peninsula was green with trees, but Corregidor had low brush scattered over the island. The most interesting to me were the many rusting ships scattered all over the bay from Corregidor to the war-damaged docks in Manila. I didn't count the number of sunken ships, but my memory guesses about 30 of all sizes, with the smaller ships only showing their masts. The dock I had been on when I got on the Nagata Maru in November 1942 to go to Japan was still there but had some bomb damage.

Many G.I. 6x6 trucks were waiting. They had the typical collapsible benches on each side of the cargo area in back. The friendly hands of the driver and his helper, with the aid of a stepladder, assisted me on the truck and my sack was stacked in the center. As soon as it was filled we took off through Manila. Manila was a mess; many buildings were gone and others lay in piles of broken rubble, even the beautiful city buildings had been blown up by the Japanese. Part of the Walled City of Manila was blown up by the American Army when MacArthur returned because the Japanese Army would not surrender; our Army's big artillery soon drove them out.

Our driver headed south for Cavite and turned off at a place called Muntinlupa, 18 miles south of Dock #17, the Military staging area for the 29th Placement Depot for all Army personnel. This was a large area with lots of mango trees where I had hidden with my tank on 10 December 1941. Today, 18 September 1945, was very different from 1941 as we were treated to free beer, candy, cigarettes, good chow, and plenty of mud to walk in!

On arrival we were given a quick physical; if we could walk and eat we were in good health! I received a tent number and that was my home for the next week or so. The object was to delay us until we gained weight, and also to supply the ship that was to take us back to the U.S. The Army cooks served lots of food, but some was so greasy I would throw it up. It was so good that I would eat it anyway and then run for the latrine (toilet). There was a notice that we could go to the Army kitchen any time and get a steak or hamburger.

The Salvation Army had ice cream and pop, which I would often get after a session with greasy food. There was also a Red Cross stand, but everything I wanted cost money, U.S. dollars. As a POW, I hadn't been issued any money yet and

Chapter 16 Freedom at last

the Japanese currency was no good. The POWs did not like this Red Cross.

As I wandered around camp I found out there were trucks going into Manila several times a day. I don't remember who was in the group with me, but I do remember walking my legs off looking at the wreckage the Japanese had made of the once beautiful city; they did it out of sheer hatred of the U.S. The marble and stone buildings they had occupied for three years were loaded with explosives and blew up minutes before they evacuated the city; they blew up all bridges right after they crossed them by order of Gen. Yamashita. The U.S. Army traced Gen. Yamashita and his troops north into the hills because of his destructive actions. At Galete Pass 7,403 Japanese and 2,065 U.S. soldiers lost their lives in the action.

The G.I. truck driver arrived and took us back to Muntinglupa in time for evening chow. I stood in line with my mess kit like any other G.I. who wants to eat.

On another day I went into Manila to check out some areas that had not been destroyed and was surprised at the high prices compared with pre-war prices. The world had just rolled on without me and I would have to come to terms with catching up 3-1/2 lost years. Nichols Field Airport was loaded with fighter planes that were not being used since the end of the war. To me, the sight was fantastic; some had huge propellers and others had two or more, some single body and others were twin bodied. I walked so much my feet cried out for rest.

I saw my friend Robert Granston one day and we talked for a few minutes. Later, I saw Bob in Seattle. He was now a Navy Captain working in Logistics.

22 September 1945

Today my traveling papers were processed. I think the "money man" must have loosened up and I drew some U.S. dollars, and then went to the clothing depot. I really needed clothes as I had only one shirt, pants, one pair of shoes and socks. The shoes were the worst as they were mighty thin after four years of hard use. The clothing distributor used the good old Government sizing methods, took one look at me and said to his assistant: "Four each 15" shirt, 32" pants, medium undershirts and shorts, large socks and, let's see your shoes. Give him size ll-D shoes." "Next! Man, wake up, you're next!" I was very glad to have clean summer khaki clothes. I pulled one each of everything, laid them on the bed, and took a shower. The G.I. bag held my summer clothes, including my dirty set of hospital clothes very nicely. They had even thrown in several cheap razor scrapers for my light whiskers and a size 7 overseas cap, plus a set of 2nd Lt. shoulder bars. By the time I finished it was chow time.

23 or 24 September 1945

I wandered into the Junior Officers Club and met Lt. Reeves of Oklahoma. We had a beer and were talking to a blonde Red Cross worker; I found out there was a letter for me from my wife dated the 18th of September. I was very surprised it had traveled so far so quickly, had been shuffled around to all the non-commissioned military staging areas, but never claimed. I was so enjoyed that I wrote in my "QUAN" (diary) book: "That's my Honey! It helps to put the 'rank' on the mail, sweetheart." The letter has been lost, but it must have had a phone number as my QUAN notes that I telephoned, but doesn't say if I got through. I know I immediately got some paper from the Red Cross and wrote to Nell.

25 September 1945

In the same evening, I received word to pack and to be ready to go to the truck area for transportation to the ship. Later, another message said to be ready at 4:30 p.m. We loaded onto the truck and it was dark by the time I got to the ship STORM KING. I met John Ryan and Clint Seymore, Zentsuji POW camp friends, who were so thrilled they undressed, walked off the pier, and dived into Manila Bay. I refused as the water was too dirty for me!

26 September 1945

The ship was loading food and pumping oil most of the day and we finally sailed out of Manila about 2:00 p.m. bound for Honolulu. The ship's rail was crowded for a last look at the many sunken ships, and also at the Bataan Peninsula and the Island of Corregidor. I stayed on for another hour or so and almost missed chow. Food was still one of the most important items in my day! When we loaded we had also been assigned specific chow times. This was not the luxury cruise ship I had been on to Manila, but I still loved it as it was on the way home. No beds, just hammocks; our schedule of life at sea was to sit, smoke, read, fire drills, abandon ship, and enjoy watching the waves, maybe see flying fish, and near Honolulu watch the dolphins swimming off the bow.

Chapter 16 Freedom at last

Chapter 17
GOOD OLD U.S.A

11 October 1945

I think this was the day that I reached Honolulu and the United States. The ship docked early in the day near Pearl Harbor and we were allowed to go ashore, but had to be back before midnight. Sam Trifilo and two more Zentsuji friends went to see the city. Since I had been there before on the way to Manila I was supposed to be the guide. Nothing looked the same! It seemed like miles to walk; we stopped to gawk at lots of things until our feet screamed for a rest so we stopped at a bar on Main Street to have a drink. I don't remember what I ordered, but it had lots of "kick." We asked for another round. Sam didn't want any more; he wanted to eat, as did another friend. The owner of the bar came over, found out we were ex-POWs and we all talked about our experiences. Sam and his friend left to see more of Honolulu and return to the STORM KING.

Chapter 17 Good Old U.S.A

The owner supplied a few more rounds while we talked.

Bar closing time and time to get back to the ship; the sidewalk was tipping me around as I zigzagged my way down the street to the boat. An Army 6x6 truck stopped; the drivers helped us into the bed of the truck, find a seat, and took us to the pier. I was next to the tail gate and put my hands on the gate. The driver yelled, "Hands off!" but it was too late. The gate went down and I fell head first onto the dock. I hit a small rock and cut my scalp which bled down my neck. I was helped up to the gang plank and into my hammock. I was "out" until about 9 a.m. the next morning when Sam came down to get me on the deck to watch the Navy Fleet head for the Mainland U.S.A. It was a big parade of ships, all flags flying, and the railings on all ships were lined with white-suited Navy personnel waving as they steamed out of Pearl Harbor. With help I managed to climb the stairs and get outside to see the last three ships leave. Then I took my throbbing head to the washroom, cleaned up a little, and went back to bed. Sam came by before noon chow, made me go to lunch where I had some milk, then back to bed. I made dinner that evening, but never again have I had a hangover like that. Probably a little concussion from the fall off the truck was making it worse.

15 October 1945

The STORM KING arrived in San Francisco. It was beautiful seeing the Golden Gate Bridge, the golden hills of dead grass, the tall buildings and the busy harbor. We were met by military buses and taken to Letterman General Hospital at the Presidio for a brief medical exam. The doctors had us strip to shorts and weighed us. I was 176 pounds; I had gained 71 pounds in the six weeks since the first food drop in Roku Roshi. The rest of the exam was to note the bullet in my neck, see if I was able to walk, or had any other injuries that prohibited my going on leave until I could be sent home. I was assigned a bed in the hospital; told where the mess hall was to eat, and given a pass.

I found my old school friend Jimmy Allison's Vallejo phone number and he came to get me and Sam Trifilo. He took us to his mother's home in Vallejo, where we visited with Charlotte and her husband, Fred Price. While I was still in high school he and Charlotte would take me with Jimmy on weekend trips such as over the Cascade Mountains to Wenatchee, to Mr. Rainier's old log lodge, etc. Fred had been a machinist at Bremerton Navy Yard, but before the war began he had been transferred to Honolulu where he sharpened turbine blades for Navy ships. They were very interested in my "trip" to the Philippines and would have talked all night, but I fell asleep talking and they gave me a bed to sleep on. Sam had given up early, but said the bed was so soft he didn't enjoy the night at all. Jimmy took us back to the Presidio the next morning.

Nell showed up the next day driving my old Plymouth Coupe; Nick Nichaelof came with her to help drive.

Chapter 17 Good Old U.S.A

I had met Nick when he was an Air Corps Observer at Clark Field, and again at Cabanatuan POW Camp when it was still possible to become an entrepreneur. I loaned him $20.00 with which he bought sugar to make candy to sell and also other items like bananas, cigarettes, and even cigars. I got my money back and bought anything I could, like bananas as my teeth were very loose from scurvy. Nick handed Nell the keys and took off to find some of his friends. She gave me the keys, but I just wasn't quite ready to drive. I did later to see if I still could. I could! We spent a few days seeing San Francisco, and then Nick and Nell took off for Seattle. I had to board the train as the Army would not let me go with them to Fort Lewis.

At Madigan Hospital (Fort Lewis), a doctor asked me if I was okay. I wasn't about to admit anything was wrong. He then gave me a week's pass. I phoned Nell and she picked me up and took me to her two-bedroom apartment at 309 16th Avenue North, Seattle. A Post Intelligencer reporter interviewed me for an hour or so, and the rest of the time I just visited a few friends. Then back to Fort Lewis for another medical exam, after which I was given Medical Leave.

I wanted to give Nell a honeymoon as we had such a short time together after marriage, and finally convinced her to go on a trip to Mexico. We drove my old Plymouth Coupe to Los Angeles where a POW friend showed us around and took us to a popular Hollywood dance hall. He pointed out a couple of movie stars, but they meant nothing to me after being out of touch for four years.

From Los Angeles we went to San Diego for a visit with Zentsuji POW, Lt. Col. John Spainhower and his wife Evelyn who gave us a very wonderful welcome. They were very special people.

Then on to Dallas to visit with Nell's Aunt Agnes and her husband and they showed us the cities of Dallas and Fort Worth as Nell had relatives in both. We spent Christmas Eve and Christmas Day 1945 with them. While in Dallas my Plymouth had a tire blowout, but was lucky to find a replacement. The tires were well worn and needed to be changed. Earl helped me find a set of four; they were substitute material, but better than the old ones. It surely felt good to be welcomed in homes of wonderful people, good soft beds, and freedom to come and go as I wished. No Japanese guards, no fleas; but I still had many nightmares of POW days.

We drove to Laredo, Texas, passed through customs into Nuevo Laredo, and on to Monterey where we spent a day visiting the brewery and drinking COLD beer in the warm weather. One of the engineers in the brewery was my mining engineer's good friend who advised us what to see in Mexico; he also advised the Mexicans who served the beer in the brewery to keep my glass filled with cold beer. Best bar I've ever been in! I was not feeling any pain when we left, but Nell did not drink much and remembered the tips.

Chapter 17 Good Old U.S.A

Mexico City, elevation 5,000 feet, was sunny and clear. One day after seeing the Emperor Maximillian museum in the middle of the city within walking distance of our hotel, which housed the clothing, furniture, etc., of the old Spanish rulers, I was surprised to recognize Zentsuji POW Mortimer Marks with his wife. That evening we hailed a taxi and using pantomime and our poor Spanish, made the driver understand we wanted to eat in a good Mexican restaurant. He finally understood and took off with a long horn blast at every intersection to inform the heavy traffic he was taking "the right of way" to get to our destination. On arrival we were surprised to look at a tall, plain, huge wooden building with no lights or grand entrance. The driver pointed to a plain door and told us to go up and turn left. We knocked on the first door and a Mexican man invited us into the crowded room. It was a big room with tables covered with white cloths. The four of us sat down and began to read the menu which was in Spanish. Mort and I began guessing what the words were as the waitress could not help. We looked around the tables and pointed to the good-looking servings and the diners round us took an interest. Soon they began suggesting what we should order. One man could speak a little English and did his best to make us welcome. When he found out we were Japanese POWs, he and some of the others ordered drinks for us and it was a most hilarious evening as we closed the restaurant.

Before leaving Mexico City we visited the Inca

ruins north of the city and I climbed to the top of one mountain of blocks with sharp rocks embedded on all sides. We were told that the Inca ruler's enemies were executed by making them climb up and then were pushed off.

Next we went on to Acapulco with Mortimer and his wife following us. We both stayed at the new hotel which looked like a typewriter as all the rooms were stepped down from the ridge it was built on. Our room was not ready, so our first night was spent in the basement on a muddy floor. They did put in a bed and planks to walk on. The next night we had a beautiful room. We stayed a couple of weeks because there was no gasoline until the next tank truck came in; but the hotel had a beautiful warm sandy ocean beach for swimming, and the hotel nearby had dancing every night as it was the hotel for Hollywood stars. I'll always regret I did not go see the famous Mexican divers plunge into the ocean from the top of the cliff.

"Mort" and his wife went on home but we drove back to Mexico City. On the way we toured Cuernavaca and visited a beautiful, old Catholic Church. The mountains had an old Spanish silver mine and there was lots of silver jewelry in the shops; we bought some. What I remember most is that the hotel restaurant served us two cups of Mexican-style coffee, dark, thick, and hot. A small pitcher of hot milk came with it; Nell poured a little in her coffee and I poured a lot to dilute the coffee. One taste! It was awful. Nell knew immediately it was goat's milk; no more coffee for us!

From Mexico City we drove to Vera Cruz, which was beautiful with coconut trees and a real tropical climate. I remember buying a stalk of ripe bananas that I really got stuffed on. From Vera Cruz to Mexico City and on to Brownsville, Texas, to look up another aunt of Nell's who had a grapefruit orchard. Their fresh grapefruit was really good. It was now late January, but it was hot here. As we started back to Seattle it became cooler. We stopped at the Grand Canyon and I particularly remember the blisters I got riding the mules to the Colorado River at the bottom and then the return. It was a beautiful ride.

At the end of leave time, I returned to Madigan Hospital at Fort Lewis to have the bullet taken out of my neck. It had been on the left side of my neck, about two inches up and almost touching my thyroid gland since my fighting days on Bataan. The doctor said I was very lucky to be alive.

Jane's good friend Maude and her husband Jess Wright lived in Richmond Beach five miles south of Edmonds and had an old house (Maude's old home) that was going to be vacant in about a month. Nell agreed it would be a good buy and we moved in after it was vacated in early 1946. We remodeled the house so we had a bedroom in the attic; I put in plumbing upstairs, and we now had an empty bedroom on the main floor.

Nell's mother, Jane Geisler, sold her home sometime

in 1947 and moved to Richmond Beach to establish a dime store in a new building about two blocks from our home and moved into our bedroom when we moved upstairs to the refinished bedroom. With Jane's and Nell's help I built the fixtures in our basement, and then moved them into the store. The last fixtures were moved at 1:00 a.m. and I went to bed. We had been working many hours to be ready and Nell stayed to arrange the merchandise and opened the store on time opening day.

Our first son Douglas James was born January 1947. Douglas died in January 1950 from polio, but diagnosis was later changed to encephalitis. On 5 February 1949, we had a beautiful red-headed girl; we named her Katherine ("Katy") Jane.

In 1948 we bought a cabin on a lot downhill from our house. I added a second story, put in plumbing on both floors, and when it was ready, we moved into it. Nell and I had the upstairs and Jane slept on the main floor. We then sold the first house we had purchased.

The dime store survived about a year, even with the addition of a small hardware section. The plain answer was that it was in the wrong location and didn't have enough traffic. A buyer for the hardware section reduced her inventory and rental charges. Jane then found a new location in Seattle west of the University and north of 50th Street and I helped her move. It was not the best location but Jane did have her own apartment above the store. As time passed, she had to

CHAPTER 17 GOOD OLD U.S.A

again vacate due to lack of business. I again helped her move to her new location in Edmonds. It was larger with a big storage area where I also built many big shelves for her inventory. This was a great location and she prospered enough to rent another store across the street for toys. At first Nell and I helped work in the store, but there was not enough profit for two families. When it became more successful, two more people were hired in her operation. Nell and I did continue to help at Christmas time. Later Jane met and married a retired ship's captain, Peter Sater, and sold the store.

After I graduated from the University of Washington on 22 June 1946, I took my first job as a full-fledged cashier in the University National Bank in the "U" District of Seattle. I worked there for a year or two, and then went to Dunn Lumber Company on Aurora Avenue and 196th Street in north Seattle; I had joined the Army Reserves and had to go to Fort Benjamin Harrison in Indianapolis, Indiana for Officer's Finance School for six months. On return I had to look for another job and became a salesman for Edward Colcock Company and using my car and selling in Washington, Oregon, Idaho, Montana, and Utah. I would be gone a month at a time, which I didn't like. In August 1946, I found a job with Johns-Manville Corporation in Seattle as a sales clerk placing orders, doing pricing information, etc.

Son Gregory was delivered 1 March 1955, in the same hospital in Seattle and by the same doctor, Dr.

Merrick, as my other two children. My family was now complete.

When Greg was about two we bought a cabin on Lake Cavanaugh, northeast of Arlington, in the mountains. I remember the day the man showed us the cabin as it had been raining. Greg walked through a big puddle of water that looked like smooth glass; how surprised he was when the water went over his tiny rubber boots. Nell and Katy helped him out and dried him off.

After improving the cabin and building a front porch, we built a dock and a float. As the kids grew older we bought a 16-foot boat with a 50 hp Mercury outboard motor. The two kids were soon water skiing like pros. Nell also skied while I piloted the boat, then she would pilot while I skied. I used only the short two skis; but once the kids had mastered the single ski, that was all they would use. They became very proficient at letting go of the tow and coasting into the float. The summers were wonderful for swimming and partying with neighbors and friends who had cabins on the lake.

About mid-July 1955 another Army Reservist and I were going to California to do summer Reserve duty at Camp Roberts. The other man was driving his car. While going down Highway 97 toward Klamath Falls, Oregon, he tried passing another vehicle when a truck came toward his in the two-lane road. He tried to get back behind the first vehicle, overcorrected and we went down the ditch into a huge rock. No seat belts back then, and I was thrown into the windshield. I broke my left arm below the elbow, four or five ribs, joint of the left knee, cuts and bruises. I was knocked out when my head hit the windshield. The two men in the oncoming truck saw us, stopped and pulled me out of the car, laid me on top of the big rock, and went to call an ambulance. I was hospitalized in Klamath Falls for two weeks and then taken to Madigan Hospital at Fort Lewis, Washington. I was hospitalized for about five months before I could return to work.

Katy was about 13 and Greg 7 and we were living at our new brick-walled home in Edmonds, Washington, when both kids begged me to take them night skiing on Snoqualmie Pass. This was a year with plenty of snow, especially at the ski resorts. I finally okayed it and they got ready with all their ski clothes, skis, and gloves. We had an early dinner and then I got my warm clothes on and put the chains in my old Chevrolet sedan. Nell didn't want to go and we took off before dark as I anticipated that chains would be required before we could get up the long hill to the top – no modern freeways yet! As I expected, chains were required and putting on cold steel chains was no snap. I stopped in a foot or so of snow off the main road, pulled out the chains, and placed them in front of the wheels. I got back in and tried to go forward enough so I could lock them on. The car only spun the tires. The car would move backward so I put the chains behind the wheels and finally got them on. I was happy to get where I could be near a heated building. I bought the ski tickets and turned the kids loose. When they got tired and cold enough, Katy and Greg would come in and warm up. After a few times the lights began blinking warning us it was time to go home and they were tired enough to go. It was great fun!

Being in Boy Scout activities with Greg was a happy time for me. I was treasurer of the troop. Greg loved the trips into the lakes and mountains so I went on a short five-mile hike to see if I could do it – I survived with blisters and the Scout Master took my picture. He pronounced me "fit" to take a 50-mile hike from Stevens Pass to the Icicle River across the Cascade Mountains. It almost did me in, but my legs got stronger even though I lost three toe nails!

In the high lake area the mosquitoes would chew you up, but fortunately, I had a mosquito net and enough space for Greg's sleeping bag. It wasn't long before the Scout Leader came over and asked if he could "stick his head in?" By daylight there were five more heads inside the net. The next day we hiked to the Icicle River where I pulled off my three layers of socks and held my hot toes in the ice water until they lost feeling. The second night after Icicle River we camped in a cozy place with moss on the ground and small fir trees to shelter us. As we were in the sleeping bags ready to sleep a young deer walked through the sleeping bags and gave us a look-over before it walked out. It was very curious and not at all afraid of us.

One of the scouts had to return early, and as we were

Chapter 17 Good old U.S.A

on our way out, I volunteered to go with him; Greg came also. We missed only one night of camping out. It was a 16-mile hike and we made the last eight miles in four hours, hiking at a steady pace, and arrived at the highway about four miles west and downhill from my car at the Stevens Pass ski parking lot. Greg and his friend stayed with the packs and I hitched a ride with a family already loaded with kids. I was sweaty and badly needed a shave from our seven days on the trail, but they picked me up anyway. We got home and really enjoyed the shower and clean beds!

In the summer of 1965 my Aunt Sylvia came visiting from Baggs, Wyoming and I took her out to see Dad at his place 1-1/2 miles out of Randle. It was the last time the four brothers and sisters were together.

In July 1963 after 22 years of marriage, Nell filed for divorce and I moved out of the Edmonds brick home. I moved to a small, dinky, sooty room, but quickly moved as I became a manager of an apartment house near Broadway in which I had bought shares. It was old and I couldn't keep up with the repairs (along with my job at Johns-Manville) so my partners and I sold. I then bought a house from Mrs. Sandal at 19321 – 84th Avenue, West, Edmonds. She left some of her furniture which we still love and use.

(Author's Note: At no time does Mr. Hummel explain why his wife divorced him and she is never mentioned again in his diary. Today if our troops come home with problems, the effect is called Post-Traumatic Stress

Disorder (PTSD). Back then, after World War II, the Korean Conflict, and the Vietnam War, there still was not a name for the problems the troops suffered.)

After Katy graduated from high school she found a job in Edmonds and once in awhile come to live with me. One of her jobs was for a man that was writing a book. He couldn't have found a better person for the job as she was very good and conscientious. I know, because during this time she typed a manuscript for me for information I needed for the Veterans Administration. The info was taken from my little diary which I called my P.O.W. Quan Book. Quan is the word we used while I was in the Philippines and it referred to any cooking in a tin can or mixing any food item to eat. I used this particular manuscript a lot while writing about my memories.

Greg was six years younger than Katy so on several summer vacations he and I would travel by car. The first of these was a trip to Alaska in August 1970 when he was 15. I had a big foam pad in the back of my Ford Station Wagon on which we would put our sleeping bags, or just blankets if it was too warm. Our route was through Canada, north along the Fraser River, then the Alcan Highway to White Horse, on to Dawson in the Yukon, and on to Fairbanks. On our way to Anchorage we made a side trip where we saw bears, moose, and the old mine where I worked for a couple of summers to earn money for college.

(Author's Note: We had five children and purchased

a vehicle with a hood, placed a mattress on the floor so the children would have someplace to sleep while my husband was driving. Later, as an electrician, he also installed a TV set so the children could watch their favorite programs.)

We went south to Kenai to visit my sister Alma and Charlie Althauser, and their son, Gordon. We fished the Kenai River for salmon and got enough to can and bring back home.

In 1971 Greg and I took a trip from Edmonds, along the Pacific Coast Highway to San Francisco, to Los Angeles, and Disneyland.

In August 1972, I decided to go to a Reunion of the Defenders of Bataan and Corregidor (ABCD) which was being held in Manila, Philippines. I invited both Katy and Greg to go with me, but neither wanted to be away from Seattle that long. It was a most enjoyable trip as my guide in Manila was Col. Ben Lerma, who had been with the Philippine Army and later a guerrilla when the Philippines fell. He remained a very special friend until his death in February 1993. Included in my tour was a visit to Hong Kong.

Dave and Eleanor Allen of Jeffersonville, Indiana also came to Hong Kong where they knew of a wonderful Chinese tailor where I ordered a suit. They also knew of the silk embroideries. I bought a "100 birds at sunset" which is still hanging in my living room, a happy souvenir.

In July 1974, I became sick and ended up having

surgery in Doctor's Hospital in Seattle. Among the "Get well" cards I received was one from my future wife, not that I was thinking of marrying again at that time! I finally got around to calling her for the Ex-POW Christmas party at Harold and Virginia Page's in Puyallup, but she had other commitments.

Johns-Manville began consolidating their many sales offices into districts; the West Coast was last. The Seattle Office Manager retired and I was given the job without title, but a good salary promotion. This lasted until October 1974 when Ray Haynes, the Officer Manager for Johns-Manville, Western Division, asked how long it would take me to fly down to San Francisco and I told him "Give me time to get home, get a ticket, and pack!" He met me at the San Francisco Airport and took me to the Corporate Office in AT&T's old rented building on Market and Main. I agreed to come down and work as a Senior Supervisor of the employees in the Sales Office. J-M had managers of various sales divisions, so just the office clerks and employees such as mail clerk, etc., would be my responsibility, plus such other duties as Mr. Haynes would decide on. He then told me to find a place to live and come down as quickly as possible. He also told me a new location was being planned away from San Francisco, so I found an old home at 2332 Boxwood Drive in San Jose, which I bought for $30,000. I assumed the G.I. Loan balance of $7,000 at 4% interest, paid $16,000 to the seller, and gave the seller a Promissory Note at 10% for the balance.

Chapter 17 Good Old U.S.A

I moved in late November 1974.

In August 1975 I came up from San Jose to go fishing with friends, Bill and Missy Wright. We came back early on my last day in Washington and I called Caroline to see if she was home. She had a house full of company as she had an "Open House" for her parents (Carl and Martha Hoger) who were visiting from North Dakota and would not be free until after 8:00 p.m. It was a happy time while I visited as I got to meet her parents and also her Dad's cousins, Walt and Thelma Richter, Spokane, WA. Walt was a brother to Carl Richter who had picked me up when I was going to Detroit to get my new Plymouth!

On 10 October 1975, the Seattle Quarter Century Club held their annual dinner-dance and my boss, Ray Haynes, asked me if I wanted to go to Seattle for the weekend. Sure would and I gave Caroline a call that evening to ask her to go with me to the dinner. It was a wonderful opportunity for her to meet the people I worked with and to get to know each other better. She met me at the hotel and after dinner, Ray and Herma Hayes took us to the Top of the Camlin Hotel to celebrate.

On the 11th we took a drive to Leavenworth and when we went through Stevens Pass I pointed out the mountain where Seventh Heaven's high ski lift was located. Greg could ski circles around me and proved it the last time I skied with him. We were coming off Seventh Heaven late in the spring season and there was frozen snow on the first down hill run. I failed to make a zigzag turn, fell and hit the ice hard with my thumb. It turned backward and was badly sprained! I never skied again.

Caroline and I were married 21 November 1975, (on the 55th wedding anniversary of her mother and father) in San Jose, California. Since Caroline had already made plans to have her vacation in Hawaii we just incorporated more stops in Hawaii for our honeymoon and visited in Honolulu, the volcanoes on the big island of Hawaii, and ended up in Lahaina where her daughter Diane and family lived.

I had promised Caroline that we would do lots of traveling but she wasn't too sure she could believe me. Our first trip was in 1976 to North Dakota where her sister Clara and Joe Schaner had a picnic for us and I met 120 of Caroline's relatives and friends. (I still don't have all of them straight but since Caroline's been gone from North Dakota so long, I think she had some trouble, too!)

Our next trip was in 1977 to the Philippines to see where I had fought in the war, and also so Caroline could see where her first husband, Adolph Richter, had spent his time. He had been a Marine stationed in Cavite in 1939; had been packed and ready to come home in November 1941 for his brother Herbert's funeral when his leave was cancelled. Guess the government knew something! He was captured on Corregidor, as was I, and spent his 3-1/2 years in prisoner of war camps in the Philippines and Japan as did I. I didn't know him till Adolph and Caroline moved to Seattle and Adolph joined our Seattle POW Chapter. Fellow travelers on this trip were Fred and Virginia Pemberton and they were travelers with us on several trips later.

In February or March 1976 Katy moved to Santa Cruz, California, and we were able to see a little more of her. Later she moved to San Francisco and began working for IBM. IBM later transferred her to Seattle, and then to Austin, Texas, where she met and married Larry Hester 18 June 1978.

I became active in National Sojourners, Golden Gate Chapter, in San Francisco in 1974. Later Chapter No. 523 was formed, which was made up of ex-POWs from all over the United States! National Sojourners consists of Military Officers who are also Masons.

The extremely polluted air in San Jose and the valley made it necessary for me to retire and move elsewhere. I waited until Caroline reached the age of 55 and she could take early retirement from Lockheed and we got ready to move to Bellingham, WA where I had a lot. Through a co-worker at Lockheed, Caroline sold our house without benefit of a real estate agent and in July 1981 Eileen became the owner of our Boxwood Drive home for $89,000. (The price escalation in California has since brought it up to $260,000, which is ridiculous for the small 3-bedroom, 1 bath house!) Eileen moved into the house in May – when we retired – and we were free to go back and forth to the house we were building in Bellingham.

Naturally, since I worked for John-Manville, we bought the shingles from a J-M dealer in the area, and had all the insulation from the factory in California in our new Chevrolet Pickup truck we had bought just for this.

Caroline wouldn't move until I also moved our twin beds. The plumber had put in the tub and toilet in the daylight; basement bath and a laundry tub in the upstairs laundry – that was our sink! We put on the siding. Eventually, we hauled ALL of our belongings from the California house in the pickup, the 8th load being all of our house plants!

We moved into our finished upstairs on Thanksgiving Day 1981. We finished the basement ourselves – except we hired the people to install the heavy drywall and some of the carpeting. We ended up with three bedrooms, family room, bath and kitchen downstairs; the house quickly became our R&R home!

People would ask us how we could leave our lovely home on the salt waters of Georgia Straits to travel, but travel we did. Our most interesting and longest trip began in September 1983 and ended in February 1984, a total of five months. College student, Paul Schumak, son of neighbors came to stay with us and then took care of the place while we were gone.

Our first stop was Bremen, Germany, to visit with Caroline's mother's cousin Ilse Harbrecht. We spent a week with her; we even took a German Senior Citizens

Chapter 17 Good Old U.S.A

Tour to Schlesswig-Holstein in Northern Germany. From there we flew to Belgium to join Globus tour bus through Holland, Germany, Denmark, East Germany, Austria, Liechtenstein, Italy, Yugoslavia, ending up in Athens.

From Greece we went to Egypt, saw the Abu Simbal, and then boarded the Hilton Nile River cruise to see the old ruins (antiquities as the tour guide told us) tombs and just beautiful scenery.

Kenya was our next stop where we had a ball shopping for our favorite souvenir, wood carvings, and going on safari. Then we went on to Johanesberg, South Africa where we made arrangements to fly to Zimbabwe and go on tour there.

Zimbabwe Airlines was not the most prompt and when we were ready to leave to make connections for Johanesberg – no airplane! Their agents were so very helpful, took us back to the Cutty Sark (the resort where we had stayed), fed us, and called for us later to put us on a plane for Harare and spend the night – all expenses paid! Here is where Caroline found her favorite souvenir – two handmade dolls dressed in costumes of the people of Central Africa – a man and woman. Even the ears of corn in the burlap bag were hand carved and wrapped with real corn husks!

Then back to South Africa where we took a S.A. Railways Tour through Kruger Park, to Swaziland (an African Homeland), to Durban. In Durban Jim Knightly (we had met while he was in Alaska in 1978 working on Charlie and Alma's boat) met us and took us to his parents' home in Pennington, about an hour's drive from Durban. We stayed with them for a week in their lovely home a couple of blocks from the warm Indian Ocean. Somehow they couldn't understand that after two months of constant travel, it was fun to just sit with them on their porch overlooking the ocean and just visit!

We got back on the tour bus at Durban to the Drakenburg Mountains north of Durban, and on to Cape Town. On the way we stopped at an ostrich farm where I rode an ostrich. Their temperature must be over 105º F as it sure felt hot. I wanted to buy an ostrich purse for Caroline but she wouldn't let me. I could believe that what she regretted was not buying a couple of bowls made of ostrich eggs? We stayed in a Cape Town at a hotel with a view of Table Mountain. We also took the cable car to the top and enjoyed the wonderful view. We also took a bus tour to Cape of Good Hope where the green Atlantic meets the blue Indian Ocean and were surprised that you could see definite colors.

We returned to Johannesburg on the Orange Train through the Karoo and the Kimberly Gold Mines. In Johannesburg we found that our reservations for Bombay via Nairobi were no good, so British Airways really had to work hard; they got us to Bombay via Sri Lanka (which our airline had not scheduled).

In Bombay we did some local tours from the Taj

Chapter 17 good old U.S.A

Hotel and then they sent us to a local tour agency which did our India and Nepal tours. It was quite an experience as the tour office was not licensed to use a credit card and they took us to a local bank where the transaction was completed in about 20 minutes. Since the bank paid the tour agency in Indian Rupees they put all the cash into a shoe box, assigned a bank guard, and back we went to the tour agency. No pictures were allowed! Our tour included New Delhi, Srinagar, Agra (the Taj Mahal), Jaipur, India, and Nepal in the Himalayas.

We spent Christmas Eve and Christmas Day listening to Christmas carols in Kathmandu, Nepal, in the highest casino in the world and the only casino between Egypt and Macau, gambling with $5.00 each with money provided by our hotel, the Soaltie Oberoi. WE LOST!

From Bombay we went to Bangkok, Thailand – it is really polluted now and there are NO emission controls on trucks there. This visit we decided to go to Chiang Mai in Northern Thailand and it was a lot of fun; cleaner, too! Then we went on to Manila, where we spent one night at the Manila Hotel in great luxury and then to Ben and Emma Lerma's lovely old home in Caloocan City. We also flew to San Jose, Mindoro with them and visited their fish farm.

Taiwan was our next stop where we stayed in the Grande Hotel, a large, old Chinese style hotel with seven restaurants and many, many shops right in the hotel. Most memorable was hiring a car and driver who took us to central Taiwan. We spent the first night in a guest house high in the mountains and it was cold! No central heating. Then we had to cross the mountains to get to the Marble Gorge. We had not driven very far, along steep cliffs when we came to a stop as there had been a rock slide and we could not go on. A very short time later we heard there had been another slide behind us and we were trapped! By then the heavy equipment was working in front of us so it helped pass the time. They cleared a single lane and we went on with not more than inches between us and the ravine several hundred feet below. The Marble Gorge was really something. The bridge was carved out of marble with the traditional marble lions guarding the entrance; even the boulders in the dry river bed were marble – AWESOME!

I have always been active in the different ex-POW organizations. After being in on the ground floor, so to speak, in Malinta Tunnel, I was Commander of the Seattle Chapter of the Ex-POWs several times; Commander of the State of Washington Chapter 1964-65, and in 1986 I had the privilege of being a delegate to the New Zealand National POW meeting in Wanganui. I decided to make it a trip of a lifetime by going to Fiji, then to Perth, Australia, to take the Indian-Pacific train across Australia, Ayers Rock, Cairns, and the Great Barrier Reef; and then tour New Zealand.

Way back in 1984 I decided that the Hummel Family History should be written so I started interviewing relatives every time I traveled, or they visited. In June 1991, I had a Sojourner meeting in Wichita, Kansas, and decided to make one last effort. I had my Dad's cousin's address in Harper, Kansas and went to see her. She helped tie the ends together and I was able to get the book written.

My son Greg was always my best inspiration and help in getting me to finish so I gave him the first copy.

Mr. Hummel, age 86, passed on to his "greater glory" on 10 May 1997, Bellingham, Washington.

Chapter 18
JAPANESE PRISON GAURDS

Lt. Col. Masao Mori was nicknamed "Blood" and "Bamboo Mori" by the prisoners. He and another guard, Kasayama Yoshikichi, whom the prisoners called "Slime," were the terror of the camp. Both were punished after the war as war criminals. "Blood" was hanged and "Slime" got a life sentence.

Some of the rest I have been able to locate are listed as CHL (confined, hard labor).

Defendant: Minemoto, Yoshinari, Cpl. Japanese Army. Tanagawa Branch POW Camp #4, Honshu, Japan. Tried 13 March 1946, Yokohama, Japan. Charge: Violation of the laws and customs of war. Did wrongfully and unlawfully kill a POW. Verdict: 10 years, confirmed.

Defendant: Kimura, Ryunosuke, Japanese Army, Tanagawa Branch POW Camp #4. Tried 13 March 1946, Yokohama, Japan. Charge: Violation of laws and customs of war. Did wrongfully kill a POW. Verdict: 10 years confinement.

CHAPTER 18 JAPANESE PRISON GAURDS

Defendant: Ikeda, Shohei, civilian guard, Tanagawa POW Camp. Tried 12 May 1947, Yokohama, Japan. Charge: Violation of laws and customs of war. Did willfully and unlawfully mistreat and abuse POWs, torture, and abuse POWs, and mistreat POWs. 15 years – hard labor.

Defendant: Ichiba, Tokuchi, Japanese Army. Tanagawa Branch POW Camp #4. Tried 13 March 1946 Yokohama, Japan. Charge: Violation of law and customs of war. Did wrongfully and unlawfully kill a POW. Verdict: 10 years confinement – hard labor.

Defendant: Hazama, Kosaku, Camp Commander, Tanagawa Branch Camp. Tried 3 February through 19 March 1947, Yokohama, Japan. Charges: Violation of law and customs of war. Permitted collective punishment on POWs, willfully and unlawfully permit and condone the unlawful mistreatment, willfully and unlawfully mistreat and failure to discharge duties as commander to control and restrain members of his command and persons under his supervision by permitting them to mistreat and abuse POWs and did unlawfully permit POWs to work and perform arduous labor while sick, diseased or physically unfit to do such labors, thereby contributing to the illness or disability of numerous POWs. Verdict: 15 years hard labor.

Defendant: Ogimoro, Yoahio Civilian guard, Zentsuji POW Camp, Shikoku, Japan. Tried 3-11 April 1947, Yokohama, Japan. Violation of laws and customs of war. Did willfully and unlawfully abuse and mistreat POWs by beating, kicking, and cuffing them; Verdict: 5 years hard labor

Defendant: Omoi, Tadeichi, Japanese Army, Tanagawa

Branch POW Camp #4. Tried: 13 March 1946, Yokohama, Japan. Charge: Violation of laws and customs of war. Did wrongfully and unlawfully kill a POW as well as beating others. Verdict: 10 years confinement.

Chapter 18 Japanese prison gaurds

Acknowledgments

I must give many thanks to Michael Miles for the wonderful Foreword he did for this book. I've known Mike and his lovely wife, Deborah, for many years and know he spent 24 years on active duty, and for that I also wish to thank him for his service to his family, our country, to us, and to our beautiful flag. It is military people like him that we owe so much.

I also wish to thank my consultant, Tom Watson, as he keeps me on planning the next book and his encouragement. It is with fond regard I recall when I first accepted this assignment for the POW story, how upset I would become and wanted to go out on my patio and scream my head off. In talking with him about it, he said to me, "Bonnie, put your heart in your pocket and get it done! I do not know anyone else who could do it the way you will!" So I put my heart in my pocket and got it done!

Acknowledgments

To all my friends and family members who encouraged me to complete the manuscript, listening to all my stories about how the POWs were treated, leaving many of them in tears; and in the process, learned how the Japanese guards treated their own people who were farmers living near the POW camps..

Author Biography

Bonnie was born in the hills of Kentucky near the Tennessee State Line. A lot of people have called her a "Southern Lady;" however, she prefers a "red neck mountain mama!"

Of 7 children she is the only one who graduated from high school and has some college in her background.

She is continually amazed at how things are now when compared to what living was like "back then."

She entered the Women's Army Corps at 18 and loved every minute of it – even the extra duty of guarding different buildings, etc. She learned right away she had a love of the United States of America, our flag, and our troops.

It is the love of the military that she decided to write military history manuscripts and very pleased at the number of books she's had published thus far.

Her writing truly began when she worked at the State Bar of California, Los Angeles office, writing articles for the Bar News particularly articles called "Cradle, Altar, Tomb."

When living in Douglas City, California, she also wrote articles for the Weaverville, Ca. newspaper. This was Bonnie's last book. After suffering a stroke some weeks before publication of this book, she passed away peacefully in her sleep this year June 8th ,2016.

www.ingramcontent.com/pod-product-compliance
Lightning Source LLC
Chambersburg PA
CBHW061638040426
42446CB00010B/1485